READING TEACHER'S HANDBOOK

Bruce A. Lloyd
Western Michigan University

LEARNING PUBLICATIONS
Holmes Beach, Florida

Library of Congress Catalog Card Number: 78-59725

ISBN: 0-918452-15-5

Copyright 1979 Bruce A. Lloyd

Learning Publications, Inc.
PO Box 1326
Holmes Beach, Florida 33509

Printing: 2 3 4 5 6 7 8   Year: 9 0 1 2 3 4

Printed in the United States of America

*Dedicated
to
Schoeneke*

Acknowledgments

This book would not have been written without major contributions from those significant other individuals who helped shape my thinking and who helped me sustain my ideas throughout the years. There are far too many to list them all, because so many contributed throughout the years it took me to finish this manuscript. There were the students and teachers in my Reading Center and Clinic at Wittenberg University. There were the students and teachers in the Upward Bound reading programs I developed both at Wittenberg University and at Western Michigan University. There were the former students in my graduate and undergraduate classes. To all of them I express my deep appreciation.

A special thanks is due Dr. Robert F. Mager whose insightful, now classic masterpiece, *Preparing Instructional Objectives* (Fearon Publishers, 1962) started it all. He put in print something I sensed, but could not express. And a special thanks to Dr. William K. Durr, author, and past president of the International Reading Association. His critique of and comments about my ideas for reading and language improvement encouraged me to continue their development. There is another special thanks due my wife who never lost faith in my ability to finish the project.

Table of Contents

1
READING I:
An Introduction

In picking up this book and reading this first page, you have made a start toward better teaching. Congratulations. You are concerned about reading. You may be worried about teaching reading skills to your students. Or, you may wonder about the reading achievement of your own children. Or, you may be thinking about how to help other teachers do a better job. And rightly so.

There is much television and radio time devoted to the theme that too many students read poorly or not at all. The newspapers, magazines, and other print media do the same. There is a great hue and cry about the abysmal state of reading proficiency for so many individuals. It also seems to be the popular thing to point out that much money is spent to improve reading. Much time and effort go into reading programs. Yet the results are less than what most of us would desire. Few people read as much or as well as we would like. School-age students often read only when they must. And we know that reading is a tool which deteriorates through nonuse.

Many sensitive, dedicated reading teachers also worry about being effective in getting students to read better and more often. They try very hard to do a good job of teaching reading. But their results with many children seem fruitless. Solutions are not always apparent. They wonder what they can do.

Moreover, many people seem to be against the educator. And nearly everyone blames everyone else. College instructors blame high school teachers, who in turn blame elementary teachers. Administrators are also blamed, so are parents and so is the community. The dialogue might go like this: An instructor at a university may say, "How is it possible that you have not yet mastered the fundamentals of the English language?" Then the high school teacher gets into the act. "Didn't you learn anything in the middle school? What kind of teaching goes on down there. If any!!"

A middle school teacher states, "My students come to me and they are so unprepared. I wish those elementary teachers would teach these kids something. After all, they have them for the entire day." The elementary teachers are also concerned because their students lack maturity: "It's no fun teaching these little ones. They can't sit still long enough for me to teach them anything. Their parents are responsible . . ."

So the elementary teacher has a conference with the parents. Usually it's the mother who shows up. And mother may be on the defensive. She may defend herself by saying, "Well, what can you expect? He's just like his father."

But, of course, this blame does not solve the problem and something must be done in the classrooms of all teachers. Yet all too few educators are really sure of themselves or sure of what to do to improve the teaching-learning situation to help students improve their reading skills and to enjoy reading activities.

As a result, there has been a frantic desperate, fad-oriented quest for *THE Cure* to all reading ills, *THE Method* that will enable all students to learn, and *THE Delivery System* that will bring all pupils up to grade level in reading achievement. This search for *THE* reading panacea has misled many educators to hop on the bandwagon of the latest untried, poorly tested, well-advertised cure-all, the "newest" approach, which would allow them to continue their present unsatisfactory and ineffective teaching procedures. As a result, some useless and even harmful reading programs came into being, rose to some prominence, reached their zenith, only to ultimately decline and be discarded because they could not do the job expected of them, the results were disappointing, the teachers were right back where they started (Heilman, 1977).

The failure of the "cure-all" concept is the logical outcome of a fundamental principle of reading instruction which states that there is no simple way to teach all reading skills to all students and that because individuals differ so widely, many approaches and methods must be used. The instructional system that suggests one single cure-all for pupil reading ills will inevitably fail because it is based on the false assembly-line premise that all learners are alike and can profit or benefit equally from the same instruction.

Probably the greatest misunderstanding of what constitutes correct, effective reading instructional procedures in any classroom stems from the hope, wish, desire, and erroneous idea that there is one process, one single procedure to reading instruction, that there is a magical reading formula which will, of itself, teach all pupils and that this approach, this method, whatever it is, will solve all reading problems.

Let's illustrate the point this way. Let's compare reading instruction and medicine. In preventive medical practices, certain procedures are suggested. If you wish to remain healthy, get a lot of exercise, get plenty of rest, eat right (avoid "junk" foods), work at a job you enjoy, and so on. So here we have a wide variety of options.

Reading achievement follows a comparable pattern: read a lot, talk about your reading, learn more vocabulary, do things to expand your ideas. These and more will help maintain high reading achievement.

There is no single way to physical and mental health. And there is no single way to reading health (achievement). Those who argue to the contrary, may be guilty of peddling nostrums. This problem is not new. For many years, respected leaders in the field of reading have spoken and written about the non-existence of a universal reading approach or method to reach all children, but to little avail. For many years, teachers have been alerted to avoid the misuse of existing reading programs and skill delivery systems (theory and methodology), to avoid misunderstandings regarding their strengths and limitations, but this also has gone unheeded. For many years, educators have been writing about the fact that there is no single reading method or procedure which will, of itself, prove to be the solution to all pupil reading problems, and again to no avail (Heilman, 1977). We can only wonder why.

POINT OF VIEW

It would seem that the fundamental responsibility for proper and effective, or improper and ineffective, use of present-day, potentially valuable reading instructional procedures rests with classroom teachers and with reading supervisors at all levels of education. It is the classroom teacher who is well prepared, or ill prepared, to cope with the reading problems of the pupils; and it is the less prepared, less perceptive teacher who erroneously believes that the materials and procedures used will, of themselves, do the teaching. Therein lies the greatest error (Harris & Sipay, 1974).

It is not so much the materials used in the reading instructional program that do the teaching, but rather what the teacher does with those materials. That does the teaching. Reading lessons and skill-building activities, the materials used, are merely the vehicle or the delivery system for learning. The potential for positive instruction and learning lies not so much in the materials themselves but how the teacher utilizes the materials with students. Consequently, the teacher is more than a catalyst. The teacher must do more than merely bring pupils and lessons together while remaining unaffected by either (McKee, 1966). The teacher must become involved, plan, organize, persevere and really teach.

But even more to the point, the teacher must properly plan and become correctly involved. There needs to be a teaching or instructional and meaning-centered orientation toward the reading skills program. Therefore, it should be understood that no reading system is, of itself, inherently good or effective; nor is it, of itself, inherently bad or ineffective. Actually, it is the effective use of the suggested procedures that makes or breaks the value of the reading instructional program itself. It is the teacher who makes the reading process viable and a joy to use or turns it into an uninspiring ritual causing pupil boredom, frustration, and a dislike for school in general and reading in particular (Spache & Spache, 1976).

The classroom teacher who is a perceptive and confident professional person can take almost any reading skill instructional program and do a credible job with it. The creative, dedicated competent teacher, who knows how to plan, who is enthusiastic and willing to put forth maximum effort, can work wonders with children. Therefore, the watchword for the teacher is: be flexible, be creative, be confident in your knowledge that you are probably doing the right thing and be prepared to work hard.

On the other hand, the uninformed, poorly prepared classroom teacher can take the best reading instructional program and misuse it to such an extent that the process of reading becomes so distasteful to pupils that they soon learn to have nothing to do with reading (Morrison & Austin, 1977). And their behavior indicates this. The symptoms exhibited by these pupils include daydreaming, loss of place, the "I don't care" attitude, and sometimes even physical illness may result. This is their way of subtly expressing their resistance to a dissatisfying even traumatic experience with reading and reading instruction (Heilman, 1977).

Frequently, the teachers who find their students behaving in these fashions either apply more forcing techniques or give up entirely and cease trying to help them read better. The forcing syndrome, wherein the teacher keeps poor readers after school, keeps them in from recess, or denies them certain privileges, rarely improves the poor reader's attitude toward reading. More than likely it has the opposite effect and pupil resentment increases, the self image deteriorates, and negative learning takes place.

For those teachers who give up on students, the results are the same. The teachers who stop trying to help reluctant pupils are usually convinced that they have done everything possible and have no recourse other than to stop wasting their time with the unteachables and use it to better advantage with those other few who perhaps can be reached. But this thinking is also in error.

Most unreachables can be reached and most unteachables can be taught if teachers would correctly apply the knowledge they already have. If teachers would believe in themselves and their own professional expertise, they could work wonders with students. If teachers would have high expectations of students and expect them to perform, most of them will do just that and meet such expectations.

THE PRESSURE SYNDROME

It should be noted that the classroom and reading teachers alone are not totally responsible for the generally inadequate use and application of what is presently known about teaching reading skills to pupils. There is a host of contributory pressures that result in this type of teacher behavior. All too frequently parents fail to treat the teacher as a professional person and they also tend to make extensive demands on the school. Moreover, they often use the reading achievement of their offsprings as status symbols to bolster their own egos and insecurities, so they must unquestionably share the blame for the results of this coersion. For example, all too frequently the uninformed parent insists that his child be taught "phonics" or "linguistics" or some similar popular cure-all because s/he read somewhere that it was "good" for a pupil. And some teachers may wilt under such pressure because they are not too sure of themselves and have little or no confidence in their reading programs as presently structured. Teachers have little faith because the reading instructional program has not been as effective as they would like it to be.

Another contributing factor in the decline of effective reading instruction can be traced to administrators and reading supervisors. They sometimes fail to provide proper leadership for teachers and fail to protect teachers from parental pressures as noted above. Moreover, they themselves vacillate under pressure and not only fail to provide proper support for teachers, but also fail to provide adequate teaching materials and facilities conducive to a sound, well-balanced reading program. They, too are not always sure of the correct way to teach pupils to become better readers and the uncertainty leads to hesitation which is ultimately disasterous for so many pupils.

But the major figures in the cluster of causes regarding pupil reading deficiency are the institutions of higher learning and the various state departments of education. More often than not our colleges and universities are at fault in their teacher education programs in general and reading courses in particular. A number of these institutions do not require even one reading methods course of their education students and the state departments of education continue the certification of teachers even if those teachers have not had a reading methods course. Others may require only one reading course for elementary teachers and none for secondary teachers. It is the rare college or university that requires more of the undergraduate education major.

And even more detrimental to the cause of effective reading instruction, more ominous to the future reading skills of pupils at all levels is the reading methods course itself. Educators at all levels should not lose sight of the oft heard student complaint that most undergraduate reading methods courses are, at best, a waste of time. The only reason these students took the course was because it was required, even so, it did little or nothing to help them understand what would ultimately be expected of them in teaching reading when they became classroom teachers (Taylor, Govatos & Lloyd, 1970). Fortunately, this situation seems to be improving (Morrison & Austin, 1977).

If further progress is to be made to increase pupil reading proficiency throughout the grades, if reading instruction is to be meaningful and effective for pupils in elementary, middle, and secondary schools, then something more must be done to cause a change. If all teachers are to be aided in thinking and assisted in realizing that reading skills *must* be taught to *all* pupils (even tenth grade biology and eleventh grade government), the procedural failures of the past should be discarded. The old established order needs to be re-examined and changed. The non-effective teachings should be eliminated. Too much of traditional reading instruction has been shown to be less than effective and too many students are doomed to second-class lives because they cannot read well.

So a fundamental change in reading methodological procedure and approach seems to be in order. What is apparently called for is a great and dramatic shift in thinking about reading and a monumental thrust in the direction of effective teaching and real learning. A radical switch is required so as to break away from the erroneous, ineffective, often degrading and traumatic experiences that pass for reading instruction in the typical classroom. To this end the present reference book is directed.

INEFFECTIVE METHODOLOGY

A modern eclectic view of reading instruction indicates beyond question that it is not a subject to be mastered as previously surmised, but rather a process for learning. It is a means whereby students become more knowledgeable, a process which combines many related skills.

In the past, teachers were erroneously concerned with single facets of reading instructional programs and thought, for example, that if only pupils knew sight words they would be good readers. Or, if they only knew phonics they would be good readers. Or if they could only read well aloud then all reading problems would be overcome. Now it is known that each of these skills, although vital to the process of reading, is insufficient by itself if a pupil is to become an independent reader (Harris & Sipay, 1974).

The sight word (visual) method, as the sole instruction program is ineffective simply because there are too many words in English. No one could realistically expect children to memorize the million plus words comprising our language. Furthermore, although the sight word method is a valuable and necessary aid to reading, it has its limitations and if a student does not learn best through the visual mode, or if he has no word attack skills, then he must resort to guessing at unknown words. This in turn, leads to failure and frustration, lack of comprehension, a poor self-image, and ultimately the decline of reading desire or interest.

The phonics (auditory) method, as the sole reading instructional program, is also limited in its utility because of the nature of the English language and the nature of the method itself. In phonic analysis, teachers are concerned with helping pupils establish the correct relationship of sounds to symbols. This is rightly so. Children need to know that the printed symbols on the page represent certain speech sounds which people use when they talk to one another. The fallacious reasoning about phonics probably lies with the assumption that sounding symbols is the ultimate goal of reading (Lloyd, 1965). If this were so, there would probably be fewer reading failures and the tasks of the teacher would be much easier, but such is not the case. Reading is more than sounding out words. Reading should also be concerned with understanding and meaning. Phonic analysis by itself rarely if ever provides meaning in words.

Teachers should teach phonic analysis so as to help pupils sound out words in the hope that those words are known aurally or are in the pupil's vocabulary of understanding or comprehension. If the student has had sensory experiences with concepts and has heard words spoken, he may be in a position to recognize the printed symbol if he sees the word and can apply correct phonics principles.

But there is a danger in too much phonic analysis. There is the danger that the reader will come to rely on or depend too much on phonics generalizations and many generalizations are notoriously failing in their utility (Clymer, 1963). Furthermore, too much phonics can cause pupils to be word-by-word readers, syllable-by-syllable pronouncers, or even letter-by-letter synthesizers, all to the detriment of comprehension and reading speed. If a student relies too much on phonic analysis, his speed of reading as well as versatility decrease. The result is that he loses the thought because by the time he has plowed through the syllables of words and the letters of words, the thought conveyed by the words and sentences has not been assimilated. He reads so slowly that the mind wanders and when this happens comprehension suffers. In this instance, the pupil has been so busy looking at the trees that he has failed to grasp the beauty of the forest. So phonics, by itself, has limitations and certainly should not be thought of as *THE* reading method, something to be taught by itself.

The same comments hold for kinesthesia alone and oral reading alone. In the kinesthetic or tactile (motor) method of teaching reading, students learn words by tracing or copying them and then trying to reproduce them from memory. Obviously, this is a time consuming task and should be used only with pupils who can be reached in no other manner. However, kinesthesia is valuable when other methods fail and it has a place in the reading instructional program.

Oral reading, once the darling of the uninformed, also has severe limitations as the sole aim of all reading instruction. For some reason, the myth continues. For some reason, teachers still conduct oral reading instructional programs of the barbershop variety (next- next) and expect pupils to be facile word callers rather than astute paragraph comprehenders (Lloyd, 1965).

Much has been written decrying the practice of having children read aloud from the same book, but to no avail. So in order to provide the necessary rationale and procedural basis, the following concepts in this book are proffered for consideration. It is hoped that an examination of these ideas will provide the classroom teacher and the reading teacher with enough suggested procedures to help him or her feel secure in breaking free from the old shackles of outmoded, erroneous, ineffective reading skill programs, and use the suggestions to aid all students.

SUMMARY

Our educational efforts in reading have failed to help all pupils reach the maximum of their potential. All too frequently teachers have been searching for something that does not exist, namely *THE BEST METHOD* for teaching reading. Materials will not do the job, but the teacher can. Failure to support teachers and to effectively instruct them are probable causes of subsequent poor student reading achievement. Teach children according to the ways they learn best, be it visual, auditory, or motor, and many reading problems will disappear. How to do just that is the rationale of this reference book.

2
READING II:
Its Meaning

Over the years much has been written about teaching reading and how to help individuals read better than they do. There are hundreds of books available to the classroom teacher and reading teacher, books which argue for this method and that, books which suggest special techniques and those which offer general suggestions for reading improvement. In fact, so much has been written that one wonders why reading problems exist for students in school and individuals out of school. We may think that there are reading problems despite the vast amount of material available. Or we may think that there are such reading problems because of all that is available and the more there is, the more confusion as to the best approaches to use for solving reading problems.

Perhaps that is precisely the problem. Too much has been written about teaching individuals to read and procedures have been obscured rather than clarified.

Maybe one more book on reading is something we do not need. But perhaps it is just what we do need because the right book at the right time may bring about the changes that are needed if teachers are to reach all individuals. An idea whose time has come is an irresistible force, something to use so that all may benefit. And it may be that this resource book will spark ideas for teachers to use as they seek to make good readers of their students.

A good place to start is at the beginning and it seems that the best beginning is to define reading. What is this process or subject which is so controversial, so difficult, so time-consuming, so expensive, and which has produced so few results?

WHAT READING IS

None of our authorities has yet agreed on a single, common definition of reading and no attempt to do that will be made here. But a close look at the act of reading can be taken and some useful definitions can be suggested for the classroom teacher and reading teacher to consider (Heilman, 1977).

One important factor to note is this: the printed word is the graphic expression of oral or spoken ideas. In the past, reading has been rather simplistically defined as nothing more than speech written down. And this is one fairly descriptive definition of reading in the initial or beginning stages. Kindergarten and first grade students and their teachers usually engage in considerable oral language activities throughout the day. Frequently, teachers will record what the children have said (speech) and write (print) the text on the chalkboard. Then the teacher will guide the students as they "read" what is written. So one beginning aspect of reading is simply responding orally to the printed symbols which were initially spoken and transcribed into print. This is, then, a reverse process. Simple enough, isn't it?

It is simple because it involves known quantities. When the students talk about what they did; watched television, visited Aunt Sophie, spent a Saturday at the art museum, the activities are something with which they have had first-hand experiences. They can talk about them because they know about them. The sensory impressions are concrete and real. And from this concrete knowledge, from this actual participation, the change to semi-concrete printed word forms expressing those same ideas is the next logical step as an outgrowth of the experience. So, yes, reading is, in part, talk written down.

But reading is more. It has to be because word recognition plays a major role in reading. And reading is more than this as well; more than mere word recognition.

Students and all who would read well need to know which printed words match which spoken words among all the million and a half words in our Americanized English language. This is the process of decoding. And it is precisely here that controversy about reading begins.

Some well-known authorities in the field are of the opinion that merely pronouncing words is reading. These well-intentioned individuals suggest that all the reader has to do is to correctly match spoken words with printed words and this is reading. If the reader says or thinks *TREE* for the printed word *TREE*, "reading" has taken place. And this is also a rather simple process, isn't it?

But what about the variations among the speech sounds (the phonemes) as so imperfectly represented by the sometimes ridiculous spellings (the graphemes) of our English language? To illustrate: try your hand at pronouncing this word: *inchoate;* and this: *synecdoche.* Did you rhyme the first word with "coat," and did you give it two syllables? Did the second end like choke and have three syllables? Nice try! If you did this give yourself 100% for effort and zero for the "test." The word inchoate has three syllables and is pronounced (in-'kō-ət). The word synecdoche has four syllables, is pronounced (sə-'nek-də-kē), and ends like key.

If you were fooled by this illustration take heart. These words were deliberately selected because they are so difficult and the purpose here is to show in some dramatic fashion that matching spoken sounds with printed symbols is frequently far from easy. Moreover, simply pronouncing words is not really reading because it does not guarantee meaning. And understanding or comprehension is what reading should be all about. Therefore, we should differentiate between mere word pronunciation and reading for meaning. We can have one without the other, but not the other without the one. This is to say, we can have correct word pronunciation, a proper matching of the sounds to the symbols, without the reader knowing what the word means. But we can seldom if ever have the reader comprehend what is read unless the word is correctly pronounced.

This presents us with another problem. Correct pronunciation of certain symbols is no easy task as George Bernard Shaw indicated many years ago. He used the letters *ghoti* to spell fish. Can you decipher this? Actually, it is quite simple: the *gh* takes the *f* sound as in enou*gh*; the *o* takes the *i* sound as in w*o*men; and the *ti* takes the *sh* sound as in na*ti*on.

To further illustrate the problem of matching symbols with spoken sound think of the digraph *ch*. It has a unique sound as in church, chore, and chap. But is also has the sound of *sh* as in chef, chateau, and chevron. Moreover, it takes the *k* sound as in choir, chord, and charisma. So is it any wonder that controversy about reading exists and teachers are constantly searching for the methods and materials which will lighten this onerous task?

Our sounds and symbols do not always match consistently. They frequently change from one word to another leaving many readers bewildered and sometimes defeated.

And correct pronunciation does not automatically confer meaning. So teachers are urged to think of reading as something which goes beyond the pronunciation of words. Actually reading is a sort of putting together of individual words whose meanings are known, and assembling the concepts so that the author's ideas or thoughts are restructured in the mind of the reader. This is the process which we can call synthesis.

So when teachers in the classroom and teachers in the special reading programs think of reading, they should think of it as a process where students or readers see, recognize and pronounce the words and then go on to think of what those words mean. This is the process of visualizing, analyzing and synthesizing. That is to say, reading requires the individual to look at words, recognize them because they have been seen before and are known, or to look at words and if they are unknown, apply word attack skills so as to approximate the oral counterpart and then put the separate word meanings together so they make sense as originally intended by the author. This is no simple accomplishment.

This then is what reading is, and, although it may be much more, it certainly can be no less. Reading is more because it requires the reader to think at higher levels of cognition. This calls for considerable sophistication on the reader's part once we go beyond the obvious, factual type reading which is so prevelent in classrooms. The following brief story will serve to illustrate this point:

> George had been marching all day. Since dawn he and his group followed the dim trail. It led through grassy lands which gave way to scrub pine trees. Then, as they slogged toward higher elevations, the trail led through a thick pine forest. As they moved deeper into it, the trail became less distinct. George wondered if he would lose it as well as the opportunity it presented. Would all this effort go for nothing?

As noted already, reading is more than mere word attack, pronunciation, and oral response. The story of George can demonstrate several levels of reading which should be a part of the definition, and which teachers should consider as they work with students. Let us begin with the lowest level and work up to levels requiring greater cognition.

Most reading authorities would probably agree that reading for facts is the lowest level of cognition requiring the least sophistication of the reader. Questions such as these would tend to bring out those facts:

- What had George been doing all day? *Marching.*

- What was he following? *A dim trail.*

- What was at the higher elevations? *A thick pine forest.*

Now, because reading is more than obtaining the obvious, let us take a look at the less obvious, but important meaning of the story. To do this we should ask a different type of question, such as the following:

- How do you suppose George feels now? *Tired.*

- Why? *From marching all day.*

- How else might he feel? *Hungry; discouraged.*

- Why? *No mention made of eating; losing the trail; etc.*

Once the reader reaches this level, the next one up is relatively simple. This calls for a type of speculation. Here the reader can go much beyond that which is given in the passage and this is where self-transposition takes place. The reader places or injects him/herself into the story and tries to become more a part of it. This step requires an even different type of question and greater cognitive skills:

- Why were George and his group following the dim trail? *We do not know. The text does not tell us.* OK. How about this:

George and his group are FBI agents and they are trying to break up a smuggling operation.

George and his group are members of a special team of scientists and they are tracking Bigfoot.

George is prisoner of a radical group and if the trail is indistinct, he will not be able to escape.

and so on.

The purpose so far in this second chapter has been to give the reader some viewpoints on defining reading. Once we know what it is, we can then begin corrective measures for those who need them.

To summarize what reading is leads us to these generalizations:

1. Reading is reconstituting talk or speech written down.

2. Reading is looking at and pronouncing printed symbols.

3. Reading requires a large vocabulary.

4. Reading requires word attack skills.

5. Reading requires the reader to get the sense of the author's message.

6. Reading requires concentration and thinking on the part of the reader.

7. Reading forces the reader to be transplanted from the present, actual site to the place being described in print. This is the self-transposition concept so frequently missing from the reading done by most readers.

Now we should take a close look at another consideration. Since we know what reading is perhaps we can find out why there are so few individuals reading to the best of their capabilities. Moreover, we may be able to discover why there are so few real readers in our society.

From time-to-time news media presentations periodically decry the sad state of reading achievement among students in school. Impressive (or frightening) statistics are cited showing how poor student performance is on reading tests. Newspaper items and feature stories describe this lack of achievement, this wasted effort, and wonder why students perform in such a fashion.

As educators, many of us take reading for granted, so much so that we may not understand why others do not read. We use reading as a tool for getting information and seldom give it a second thought because it comes automatically. As teachers and because we are educated, it seems natural for us to turn to the printed word for diversion, relaxation, enjoyment, instruction, knowledge and information.

What could be more logical than reading to find facts, figures, names, dates, times, and places when we are curious about something? What could be more sensible than picking up a how-to-do-it book on whatever needs repairing around the home and do it yourself. So there are many reasons for reading, the practical as well as the esthetic. But there are many who do not read and there are many who cannot read.

THE DO NOTS

Let us take a look at the many individuals who can read, but do not. Why is it that so many choose to do just about anything else instead of reading? Has all that "education," all that time, effort, and expense gone for nothing? Probably not, but why don't many individuals read?

Perhaps part of the answer lies in what reading means or meant to the reader during the good old school days. It is quite possible that reading is considered to be something that only a sissy, egg-head, or girl does. The child may have been raised in a "man's" environment (whatever that is) where reading was not encouraged but discouraged. The home environment plays an important part in a reader's achievement and, if appropriate support is lacking, little reading takes place.

Another possibility is the way the reader interprets reading. Is reading nothing more than page after page of workbook exercises? Some students think so because that is what they did for "reading." If this is all an individual does during the developmental reading program in school, then it is easy to understand why such a negative and erroneous interpretation of reading was formed. What could be more boring than to fill in blank spaces on work sheet after work sheet for an hour a day, day after day especially in the early formative years of schooling.

Perhaps some individuals do not read because they were made to feel inferior and worthless as people. This can come about deliberately or inadvertently, but it is real and it can have a lasting effect on the reader. The teacher is usually responsible for this and begins by dividing students into reading groups. They may be the peacocks, the robins and the buzzards. Who wants to always be a buzzard? Or the teacher could use words that hurt the child's ego and do other things to cause feelings of inferiority to develop. So there are many reasons why those who can read choose not to do it.

THE CANNOTS

Those individuals who cannot read present real problems for the classroom/special reading teacher. The causes of this situation are far from simple and actually focus on the individual as a person. That is to say, for each one who cannot read, the reasons are within that person and must be discovered so appropriate therapy can take place. Therefore, it is difficult to generalize and teach the non-reader in a mass-produced assembly-line type program. Those who cannot read need individual instruction initially and the regular classroom teacher may be hard-pressed to provide it.

In trying to answer the question as to why a person cannot read there are probably as many correct responses as there are non-readers. Fortunately, there are very few who are totally illiterate. Most individuals usually can read something even if it is at a primer level. They do know some words and can look at those words and pronounce them. And this skill brings us to one descriptive factor: the poor reader has a limited vocabulary of words recognized at sight. The non-reader has no sight recognition vocabulary.

Sight vocabulary or words recognized instantly is one important accomplishment of any good reader. The larger the sight vocabulary the better the reader. Conversely, the smaller the sight vocabulary the poorer the reading.

Another reason why one may be a non-reader is to be found in the knowledge of sound-symbol relationships. The person who cannot read, not only has no sight vocabulary, but also has no understanding of why words are pronounced the way they are. The symbols (letters of the alphabet and letter combinations) and the sounds represented by those symbols are unknown or meaningless to the non-reader. If the would-be reader sees a word and has no concept of the sound-symbol relationships then he or she will remain a non-reader because he has no method of attacking the word to produce the appropriate sounds.

So we have two major reasons why those who cannot read do not read. The first is lack of sight vocabulary and the second is lack of means to unlock the sounds of the printed symbols. There are these and more, but they serve to illustrate why non-readers remain non-readers. Oftentimes, they are simply not aware of these needed skills and oftentimes teachers take these skills for granted. That is, teachers assume such knowledge on the student's part so appropriate instruction is not forthcoming.

In this handbook for classroom/reading teachers we will assume nothing. We will take nothing for granted. Instead, appropriate testing procedures will be suggested for all pertinent skills so that none will be missed. The testing sequence and related therapy program will leave nothing to chance.

So, get ready. Get set. And go to the next chapter. In Chapter 3, some important ideas about testing are suggested. Some ideas are new and some are not so new, but all of them are valuable and worth putting into practice.

3
TESTING:
The Place to Begin

AN INTRODUCTION

The first step in any reading instructional program is to find out where the students are in their reading achievement. Whether we are concerned with a developmental reading program or a corrective reading program, it is important for the teacher to know the reading/language skill proficiency status of each student. There are several dimensions to such testing as noted below, but this is the place to begin.

Testing is necessary in reading just as it is in, let us say the field of medicine or health care. In order to help the patient, the medic has to first find out what is wrong then prescribe, and the same is true for reading instruction. So classroom teachers and reading teachers will no longer need to wonder how to begin an effective reading instructional/therapy program in their classrooms or clinics. No longer will they need to ask questions such as, "Where do I start?" and "What reading skill instructional materials shall I use with my students?" The answers to these questions are already known: Begin with the student and start where s/he is. Use instructional materials that will do the jobs effectively.

And for this an adequate diagnosis is required. So *testing* is the first step and the purpose of this chapter is to offer some suggested guidelines and ideas that will serve to help teachers find out about the reading strengths and deficiencies of students.

The classroom teacher and the reading teacher have several diagnostic/testing options available for determining the reading strength/deficiency status of their students. There are many, many testing instruments available for this purpose and teachers should give these options considerable thought before deciding which to use.

For the most part, there are four broad-based categories of tests or diagnostic instruments available for use by teachers. The first category is that of the standardized, norm-referenced reading achievement tests. The second category consists of non-standardized, informal, teacher-made tests or the informal reading inventory (IRI). The third category is called the criterion-referenced tests (CRT), and the fourth category refers to measuring the student's learning modality or the way s/he learns best. Let us now look at each category in a little more detail.

STANDARDIZED, NORM-REFERENCED READING ACHIEVEMENT TESTS

These are commercially prepared tests which, for the most part, do an adequate job of classifying student reading performance on the basis of national norms (or at least large scale norms). They have advantages and limitations as do all tests and teachers should know about their values as well as their weaknesses. Although our purpose here in this reference book is not to describe such tests in detail, there are some important considerations for teachers to note.

Typically, the commercially prepared, standardized reading tests fall into two classifications: 1) individual tests, and 2) group tests. The individual test is usually administered by the reading teacher because s/he probably has taken a course in testing and has learned how to administer, score, and interpret the results. As the category indicates, these tests are administered on a one-to-one basis.

Some of the individual reading tests that enjoy a good reputation are:

1. Donald E. Durrell. *The Durrell Analysis of Reading Difficulties.* New York: Harcourt, Brace, Jovanovich.

2. George D. Spache. *Diagnostic Reading Scales.* New York: McGraw-Hill, 1972.

3. Arthur I. Gates & Anne S. McKillop. *Gates-McKillop Reading Diagnostic Tests.* New York: Teachers College Press, 1962.

As noted above, there are many good individual reading tests, that is to say, reading tests that are administered on an individual basis, but our purpose here is not to note them in detail. That has been done so very well elsewhere and you may want to read the excellent critiques provided by George D. Spache in *Diagnosing and Correcting Reading Disabilities.* Boston: Allyn and Bacon, Inc., 1976.

You may also want to read these texts:

1. C. Mauritz Lindvall & Anthony J. Nitko. *Measuring Pupil Achievement and Aptitude* (2nd Ed.). New York: Harcourt, Brace, Jovanovich, Inc., 1975.

2. John Salvia & James E. Ysseldyke. *Assessment in Special and Remedial Education.* Boston: Houghton-Mifflin Company, 1978.

Group reading achievement tests are usually administered by the regular classroom teacher because no special training is required. The manual of instructions or test guide explains in great detail how teachers should proceed and if s/he follows the directions carefully, their results will usually be satisfactory. It is important to note here that the resulting scores obtained on these tests usually indicate the performer's frustration level. Therefore, the teacher should not use that score as a reading placement index, but rather amend it according to the following considerations. To find the *instructional* reading level go down one to one and a half placements, and to find the *free* or *independent* reading level go down two to two and a half grade placements. For example, if a student tests out at 6.5 in comprehension of reading material, start instructing him/her at the 5.0-5.5 level and give free or *independent* reading material at the 4.0-4.5 level of readability difficulty.

Some of the group reading tests that enjoy a good reputation are:

1. Arthur I. Gates & Walter H. MacGinitie. *Gates-MacGinitie Reading Survey.* New York: Teachers College, Columbia University. (These surveys range from Kindergarten reading readiness on through Grade 12.)

2. *Iowa Silent Reading Tests.* Harcourt, Brace & World. (These tests range from Grade 4 through 14.)

3. *Metropolitan Achievement Tests: Reading.* and *Stanford Achievement Tests: Reading.* New York: Harcourt, Brace, Jovanovich. (These tests can be used from 1st Grade on through Grade 6.)

Space does not permit a longer look at standardized reading achievement tests, nor is it the purpose of this text to go beyond what has been noted. So for the teacher who wants to know more about which standardized commercially prepared norm-referenced tests are available, the following resources should be consulted:

1. Oscar K. Buros (Ed.). *The Sixth Mental Measurement Yearbook.* Highland Park, New Jersey: The Gryphon Press, 1965. (Also, look at his *Reading Tests* and *Reviews,* 1968.)

2. Eldon E. Ekwall. *Diagnosis and Remediation of the Disabled Reader.* Boston: Allyn and Bacon, Inc., 1976.

3. George D. Spache. *Diagnosing and Correcting Reading Disabilities.* Boston: Allyn and Bacon, Inc., 1976.

4. Miles V. Zintz. *Corrective Reading* (3rd Ed.). Dubuque, Iowa: Wm. C. Brown Company, 1977.

For those teachers who want to know more about the general nature of testing and the problems arising therefrom, these references will be of great value:

1. Walter H. MacGinite (Ed.). *Assessment Problems in Reading.* Newark, Delaware: International Reading Association, 1973.

2. William E. Blanton, et al. *Measuring Reading Performance.* Newark, Delaware: International Reading Association, 1974.

INFORMAL READING INVENTORIES

A second diagnostic category to consider when testing students to discover their reading strengths and weaknesses is that of the informal, teacher-made variety. These tests are usually referred to as the Informal Reading Inventory or IRI and have several advantages not inherent in the formal, standardized, norm-reference tests. The Informal Reading Inventory has the advantage of being easily constructed. Some reading authorities say that all a teacher needs is a series of basal readers and then to follow through by having a student read a paragraph or so from each level until s/he can no longer read with ease and comprehension. Such a procedure will give the teacher enough information to properly place a student for reading instruction. Well, this is certainly an advantage and there are others, but a more sophisticated IRI should be constructed by the teacher and it is easily administered to students. Such testing is usually done on an individual basis. That may be a disadvantage to the busy teacher who has many students to test. But the IRI presents less of a threat to students because the test or diagnosis situation is less formal and less rigidly structured than the standardized test situation.

The informal reading inventory can take many forms and the actual content should depend on what the teacher is attempting to discover. So, the content is flexible and different teachers will have different types of inventories. Some IRI will contain many different kinds of informal tests and other IRI will be less complete, but all should be comprehensive enough to satisfy the dignositic needs of the teacher.

Teachers and diagnosticians are cautioned to take nothing for granted as far as student reading knowledge and achievement are concerned. That is to say, do not assume that a student knows a skill and instead of making such an assumption, test the individual to determine the degree of proficiency (or lack of proficiency) s/he has acquired. Then build the reading instructional program based on these test findings. We should think of diagnosis as a template or guide to instruction because it is a kind of map showing us where we are and where we are going. And, once we know where we are going, we will know when we have arrived.

There are many reading skills and reading related behaviors for which the teacher/diagnostician should test. These range from simple to difficult in the three major learning modalities (visual, auditory, and motor). Teachers need to assess the visual discrimination skills that students possess as well as their auditory discrimination skills. Teachers need to know about the vocabulary knowledge each student has and how accurate or well the reader comprehends print material.

And to assist in this effort, the following Informal Diagnostic Reading Tests (IDRT) are made available to you. Each subtest is described in detail so that the teacher/diagnostician can construct it if necessary. Moreover, the entire inventory is reproduced in the appendix so as to save time and all that is necessary is to affix each test on a piece of heavy cardboard. If you wish, you could dry mount each subtest and then laminate for greater permanence.

THE INFORMAL DIAGNOSTIC READING TEST

The material presented on the following pages has been tested in a clinical situation and has proven to be of great value in pin-pointing student reading problems.

From these tests, classroom teachers and reading teachers will discover much valuable information about the reading skill proficiency/ deficiency of each student. Almost all of the tests can be administered on a group basis if the teacher chooses to do so. But it is recommended that the testing be carried out on an informal and individual basis, especially so for the reading teacher who tests students and works on a one-to-one basis in the reading room.

Test the students as indicated on each subtest. For example, if you administer the first subtest (1. Visual Discrimination I) on a group basis, flash the card for one second and have the students draw the one that does not belong or the one that is different. The dialogue could go something like this:

> Boys and girls, I need to know some information about you so I am going to ask you to do something for me. Listen carefully and do just what I tell you.
>
> Look at this card (hold the card for all to see) and draw the one that does not belong. Draw the one that is different. Put your drawing by number one on the answer sheet.

(Pause)
Now I am going to hold up another card. Look at it and draw the one that is not the same. Put your drawing by number two. You should have drawn the one that is different.
(Pause) . . . etc.

Continue in this way until all four cards in the first set have been presented and students have responded. Then go on to the second subtest (2. Visual Discrimination II). Proceed in the same manner. Do the same for the other subtests, then collect and score the answers.

1. **Visual Discrimination I.** Make 4" x 11" flash cards containing simple geometric forms such as circles, squares, diamonds, etc. and have students draw the one that does not belong. This is a test of gross visual discrimination. Four of these visual discrimination subtests are sufficient to test for proficiency in this skill. See Appendix A for the example already prepared for you.

2. **Visual Discrimination II.** Make 4" x 11" flash cards containing letters of the alphabet such as "b b m b b" or "s s s h s" and have students draw the one that does not belong. This is a test of medium difficulty in visual discrimination. Four of these are sufficient. (Appendix B)

3. **Visual Discrimination III.** Make 4" x 11" flash cards containing alphabet letters that are more difficult to distinguish such as "h b h h h" or "m m n m m" or "o o o o a" and have students draw the one that does not belong. This is a test of fine visual discrimination. Four of these is sufficient. (Appendix C)

4. **Letters of the Alphabet I.** Check to find out if the students know the letters of the alphabet. Have them write the letters in sequence as fast and as clearly as they can. Allow younger students about a minute and older students about a half minute. Or use the alphabet test given in Appendix D. If you use

this test, you should plan to administer it individually.

5. **Letters of the Alphabet II.** This is a check to find out if students know the letters of the alphabet in sequence from a given point. Make 4" x 4" flash cards of letters such as "b d f l p t w" and have students write the next two letters which follow the letter they have seen. (Show the letter "f" and students should write "f-g-h", etc.) Select four letters for this subtest. (Appendix E)

6. **Letters of the Alphabet III.** This is a check to learn whether students know the letters of the alphabet before and after a specific letter reference point. Make 4" x 4" flash cards of letters such as "c g k n r v" and have students write the letters that come before and after the letter they have seen. (Show the letter "k" and students should write "j-k-l", etc.) Select four letters for this subtest. (Appendix F)

7. **Auditory Discrimination I.** *Initial Consonants.* Say a series of words all of which begin with an initial consonant (ball - bad - bark - bird - box) and have students write the letter (b) that represents the initial sound. (Retest with "d - f - h - l - m", etc.) Have students write another word that begins with the same sound. Four trials are enough here.

8. **Auditory Discrimination II.** *Final Consonants.* Say a series of words all of which end with the same sound (bat - mit - lot - fat - hit - mut) and have students write the letter (t) that represents the final sound. Have students write another word that ends with the same sound. (Retest with other final consonants "m - p - s", etc.) Four trials are sufficient.

9. **Auditory Discrimination III.** *Initial Consonant Blends.* Say a series of words all of which begin with the same initial consonant blend (slip - slay - slam - slot) and have students write the letters (sl) that represent the initial sounds. (Retest with "br - st - gr - pl", etc.) Have students write another word that begins with the same sound. Four trials are sufficient.

10. **Auditory Discrimination IV.** *Initial Consonant Digraphs.* Say a series of words all of which begin with the same initial consonant digraph (chat - charm - chip - church) and have students write the letters (ch) that represent the initial sound. (Retest with "sh - th".) Have students write another word that begins with the same sound. Four trials are sufficient.

11. **Auditory Discrimination V.** *Phonograms* (word families). Say a series of words all of which rhyme and have the same phonograms (bang - sang - rang - clang) and have students write the letters of the sounds (ang) as best they can. (Retest with "ot - ight - ake".) Have students write another word that rhymes or has the same phonogram or family ending. Four trials.

12. **Auditory Discrimination VI.** *Syllabication Skills.* Say four multisyllable words and have students write the number of syllables they hear in each one (paper - inchoate - properly - somewhere) (auditory - familiar - consonant - vocabulary) (between - everyday - exactly - standardize). One set of four trials is sufficient.

13. **Auditory-Visual Discrimination I.** *Phonetic Spelling.* Give students a spelling test using nonsense words and have them write the sounds they hear. Explain to them that these are, indeed, nonsense words and they are to write what they hear as best they can. Say "vap - gog - vill - rem or intervent - bioclam - trabnik - selpat." Give credit for phonic accuracy of spelling. A good approximation should be accepted. Use the eight nonsense words given above.

14. **Auditory-Visual Discrimination II.** *Long Vowel Sounds.* Have students write the vowel letters (a - e - i - o - u) on their papers. Explain that when the vowel letter says its name it has the long sound. Say a series of words and have students note which vowels they hear.

Say TRY - students should write (or say) i (long i sound)
Say BEAT - students should write (or say) e
Say SO   - students should write (or say) o
Say CAKE - students should write (or say) a
Say CUTE - students should write (or say) u

15. **Auditory-Visual Discrimination III.** *Short Vowel Sounds.* Have students again write the vowel letters (a - e - i - o - u) on their papers. Explain that these vowel letters may have different sounds in some words and that *apple* has the sound of *a*, but it is short and different from the long sound. *Bet* has the short *e* sound. *Sit* has the short *i* sound. *Not* has the short *o* sound. *Rut* has the short *u* sound. Say a series of words and have students note which vowels they hear.

Say RUT - HUM - FUSS   - students write (or say) u
Say APPLE - SAD - RAT - students write (or say) a (short a sound)
Say SIT - HIM - BIB   - students write (or say) i
Say BET - MEN - FEND   - students write (or say) e
Say NOT - BOND - ON   - students write (or say) o

16. **Auditory-Visual Discrimination IV.** *Prefixes - Roots - Suffixes.* Make 4" x 11" flash cards containing words with roots and affixes. Have students copy the words, underline the root word twice, and the prefix or suffix once. Use words such as import, submarine, portable, remake, placement, formless, transportable, replaceable, nonsense, and disassembling. (Appendix G)

17. Construct a large letter "b" out of cardboard. Make it about an inch thick so there is a third dimension to it. Then have students look at it in the various positions "b d p q" and write what they see. If a student is having special difficulty with this, give him the letter and have him learn the different posi-

tions of the letters. Let the student practice by manipulating the letter and have another student monitor that practice as a check for accuracy. Retest after a suitable period of time has elapsed.

18. **Administer the Basic Sight Vocabulary Test, Part I.** Use the test as given in Appendix H. This contains the first 100 words. You may give the test in one of two ways, depending on whether or not you are testing a group or an individual.

    If you give the test to an individual, you will need a copy and so will the pupil. Simply have him read off each word in a row and as he does so, record the correct responses by making a check mark and the errors by writing in the word as said by the pupil. When the student has attempted all words on Part I, this phase is completed and they are ready for Part II.

    If you give the test to a group, each student will need a copy and you may proceed as follows: read one word in each row and have the students underline the word you said. When Part I has been completed, students are ready for Part II.

    Score the test for accuracy and also for types of errors. If a student misses more than twenty-five percent, he should be helped to learn the words missed. Print the words on 3 x 5 index cards and have the student learn the words with the aid of a helper.

19. **Administer the Basic Sight Vocabulary Test, Part II.** This will be found in Appendix H, and Part II contains the last 100 words on the list. Follow the directions as given in step 18 noted above.

20. **Administer the Clozure test pages to students.** This material will be found in Appendix I. Begin with the first selection and have the pupil read the passage silently. As he reads he should be able to comprehend the passage and fill in the missing word.

After the student has successfully completed the first selection, have him attempt the next one. Continue this until he can no longer understand what he is reading. Seventy-five percent accuracy is acceptable for each *Clozure* selection.

The student may say the word orally or he may write the missing word in the blank space. You may wish to have him write the answer on a separate sheet of paper and this is also permissable.

Many students may wish to read the entire selection first in order to have an overview of it. Then they can go back to the beginning and insert the word that fits the context. Other students may want to read several sentences before responding. This is the correct way to proceed because it indicates that students are using context clues and this is what they should do.

Go as far with *Clozure* as the student is able to go. He may be able to perform well on all selections or just one or two. Whatever he does indicates his present reading achievement. This, of course, is what the teacher needs to know so that subsequent plans can be made to help the student progress in reading.

Be flexible in scoring because there are several possible answers in most instances. If the response makes sense, then consider it correct.

Directions: How to use the *Diagnosis* page.

Score each subtest and enter the raw score in the raw score box next to each subtest. Change the raw scores to percent scores and enter them on the Diagnostic Profile. Connect the points with straight lines for the Reading Profile At a Glance.

Interpretation:

The subtests show performance in the fundamental skills students need in order to read well. A profile line graph of seventy-five

(75) percent or better would indicate satisfactory performance. The skills where deficiencies exist are seen at a glance and this is where instruction should begin. Teach students the skills they need to know and do this on the basis of findings from the tests.

There will be more on this point in the next chapter.

DIAGNOSIS
Informal Diagnostic Reading Tests for Teachers

Student's name _____ Date _____

Grade _____ Sex _____ IQ _____ CA _____ Birthdate _____

Teacher's name _____ School _____

Subtests	Raw Score	Profile-At-A-Glance
		0 · · · · 25 · · · · 50 · · · · 75 · · 100
1. Visual I (ooo▲o)		
2. Visual II (bbmbb)		
3. Visual III (hbhhh)		
4. Alphabet I (sequence)		
5. Alphabet II (f, , ,)		
6. Alphabet III (, k,)		
7. Auditory I (Initial Consonants)		
8. Aud. II (Final Consonants)		
9. Aud. III (Initial Cons. Blends)		
10. Aud. IV (Initial Cons. Digraphs)		
11. Aud. V (Phonograms)		
12. Aud. VI (Syllabication)		
13. Aud-Vis. I (Phonetic Spelling)		
14. Aud-Vis. II (Long Vowel Sounds)		
15. Aud-Vis III (Short Vowel Sounds)		
16. Aud-Vis. IV (Pref.-Roots-Suff.)		
17. Letter b position		
18. Basic Sight Test I		
19. Basic Sight Test II		
20. CLOZURE I		
21. CLOZURE II		
22. CLOZURE III		
23. CLOZURE IV		
24. CLOZURE V		
25. CLOZURE VI		

Summary of Observations:

Note: This form may be reproduced for teacher classroom use.

Figure 3.1

CRITERION (OBJECTIVE) REFERENCE TESTS

A third diagnostic category to consider when testing students for reading achievement strengths and weaknesses is the criterion reference test or the objective reference test. This type of test has many advantages and only a few disadvantages. Much has been written about this type of test since the publication of Robert Mager's classic contribution *Preparing Instructional Objectives* (Fearon Press, 1962).

Such tests are designed primarily to provide the kind of information about student's reading strengths and deficiencies, information that can be rather readily related to specific objectives (standards) or criteria deemed important by the school. Criterion or objective referenced tests use the curriculum as the expected measure of performance and from such tests the teacher can find out how well the students perform. Mastery of skills is the goal of the school and the CRT indicates the degree (or percent) of achievement or knowledge possessed by each pupil.

Criterion Reference Tests are designed by classroom teachers (or special reading teachers) and should be so constructed that they require the pupil to produce an accurate response rather than merely recognizing or selecting (sometimes guessing) which one among several choices is correct. There are six (6) important elements in a performance objective and, because performance objectives are used as the guide to the CRT, these six elements should be know to those who construct such tests.

A viable performance objective will state:

1. Performer - Who the performer is.
2. Behavior - How the performer is to act or behave.
3. Object   - What the object of the behavior is.
4. Time   - When or by when the behavior is to occur.
5. Measure   - How the behavior is to be measured.
6. Criterion - How well the performer is to behave.

We need behavioral objectives because we need to know what we are trying to teach our students. We need something concrete to which to tie student achievement and this is what the CRT is designed to do. The major advantage of the objective or criterion referenced test is that it gets directly to the point of the individual student's performance vis-a-vis the behavioral objectives which are deemed important for a specific school or school sytem or area of study.

In order for the classroom teacher and reading teacher to teach to student's individual reading strengths and deficiences, this type of test seems to provide the best measure because the instructional program is based on the weak performance information which shows how well, or how poorly the pupil is doing, they (the teachers) can plan an effective corrective therapy program.

A major problem facing many teachers is that of test availability. Although there are such tests presently available, they are few indeed when compared with the number of standardized norm-referenced reading tests. So teachers will probably need to make their own. One of the best sources of information is *Accountability: A Management Tool for Teachers*, by Chauncey W. Smith and Reuben Chapman. It is published by the State of Michigan Department of Public Instruction. This book explains the step-by-step process through which teachers should go when constructing these tests.

TESTS OF LEARNING MODALITY

Although this is not a new idea, not too many classroom teachers and reading teachers are aware of the learning modality concept. Briefly stated, the theory offers teachers the intriguing idea that students learn in different ways depending on their own unique capabilities. That is to say, students learn in one of three ways or a combination of one or more of the three ways. One way for us to learn is through the visual (v) mode. Another is through the auditory (a) mode, and the third way is through the motor (tactile-kinesthetic) approach which involves a "hands on" muscle-synapse mode. So teachers need to know how their students learn best, whether it is by the visual, auditory, or motor approach, and then plan and organize the reading instructional program to meet the student's learning modality or preference.

It should be noted again at this point that the intention here in this reference book is not to have the reader become involved in the learning modality debate, nor is it to provide an in-depth discussion of learning modality theory. These are available elsewhere as noted. (See Ekwall, Spache, and Zintz.) But our purpose is to note the existence of the concept and to give some specific, concrete ideas for the classroom teacher and reading teacher to use with students.

The reason for using a modality strength test is as simple as this: perhaps the student is a poor reader because s/he has been taught by the wrong approach. If a student is a visual learner and has been taught by an approach that is primarily auditory in nature, then the student may not learn efficiently or effectively. The usual results are failure and frustration and the pupil falls further and further behind in the work. This brings on more frustration and failure, etc., etc. It is a viscious circle of negative learning experiences.

THE VAM TEST

To alleviate the problem noted above, the teacher should plan to use a visual-auditory-motor test of pupil learning modality. One of the best known tests available is the *Learning Methods Test* (Mills, 1970). As with all tests there are advantages and disadvantages, strengths and weaknesses and the classroom/reading teacher will need to weigh all factors carefully before deciding whether or not to use it.

The *Learning Methods Test* is administered on a one-to-one basis so it is time consuming and inefficient as far as the regular classroom teacher is concerned. The reading teacher, on the other hand, may find it to be a more valuable addition to the testing procedures usually employed. Frequently, the individual approach helps the reading teacher gain rapport with the student and this can positively affect the entire testing/therapy program.

Because there are some real problems in using the *Learning Methods Test,* the classroom teacher and the reading teacher may want an alternative learning modalities test. To this end the *Visual-Auditory-Motor (VAM) Test* is made available and described in the following paragraphs.

In using the *VAM Test* teachers should be ready to quickly praise a student for accomplishment, and also to minimize the lack of success the pupil may experience. The following description explains what the diagnostician should do in order to 1) construct each test, and 2) use each test. Let us begin by testing the visual mode. In using this process we help students learn words through the use of picture clues and the printed word − a simple approach to word recognition. These are the directions for making and using the tests.

This procedure is to determine whether pupils are *visually oriented* or learn best through *visual methods.* Start by using pictures of common objects − table, chair, desk, car, bread, etc. Mount the picture on a piece of cardboard and also mount a 3 x 5 card with the name of the object *printed* on it, on the cardboard.

Then construct several cards (3 x 5) with words printed on them, one of which is the word to be learned. Have the pupil study the picture and the word printed below it on the 3 x 5 card. Then give the pupil the set of cards and find the correct word that matches the key pictured word.

Initially, the pupil may use the picture and the key word and compare visual forms if necessary. Then have him try to select the key word from among the other words without the use of the picture clue. Be sure to shuffle the cards after each trial. Allow the pupil to have several trials before presenting the words alone. Then present the words alone and find out if he selects the correct word from among the words in the group. If the pupil does not succeed, go over the procedure again for a *maximum* of *three* "teaching" lessons. If the child still fails at the task, it is probable that he is not *visually oriented* and will *not* learn best through teaching methods that are primarily visual in nature.

If the pupil does select the correct word, indicating that he probably knows it, then stop at this point and go on to another activity for 5-10 minutes. When that time has elapsed, present the words to the pupil again and determine if he can *recall* the correct word, selecting it from among the others.

Another test to use is the auditory (phonic) approach and it is used to determine whether students learn best through hearing and listening. In testing pupil's auditory mode, teachers will determine whether a pupil has the ability to associate the speech sounds (phonemes) with the written or printed word or letter (grapheme). In this test, teachers will attempt to discover if the pupil can blend letter sounds (to sound out the word) and correctly pronounce a word. Here is how to proceed.

Select consonants that lend themselves to extended sounding such as m = mmm, n = nnn, r = rrr, s = sss, f = fff, v = vvv, and avoid letters such as b, d, h, l, etc., since these are difficult to pronounce in isolation. B may end up as buh; d as duh; etc. Avoid the letter c initially because it has no sound of its own, and may be pronounced as k (can, come, etc.) or as s (city, cent, etc.). Avoid the letter g for the same reasons.

Using the consonants whose sounds can be extended (f, m, n, r, s, v) show the pupil each letter singly as printed on a flash card. Begin the test by taking one letter (e.g., f), showing it to the pupil and saying a series of words that begin with it (fan, farm, fern, feet, fate, fast, favor, etc.). Or, use the letter m and say a series of words that begin with its sound (e.g., man, men, moon, more, move, might, mar, etc.) Stress the initial sound by extending the pronunciation fff, mmm (fffan, fffarm, fffern, mmman, mmmen, mmmoon). Then have the pupil say these words one at a time as they are pronounced by the examiner. (Examiner: mmman, Pupil: mmman, etc.)

When this is successfully accomplished compliment the pupil. Go on to the next step which is to have the pupil say words that begin with the initial consonant being tested. Say, "Can you say some other words that begin with the letter f, the same as fan, farm, fern?" If the pupil responds correctly go on to do the same thing with the other letters (f, m, n, r, s, v), using two or three more of them in the same manner.

The next step is to test the pupil's knowledge of vowel sounds. Show him flash cards of the vowels (a, e, i, o, u). Explain that there are two major sounds (short, long) and that you will be working with the short sound first (fan, man, nan, ran, sand, van).

Using the word fan or man, extend the short vowel sound faaan, maaan, so that the pupil can hear it. Have him repeat the words as they are said in this extended manner. Then have him say words that have the short A sound in the medial position.

Repeat this procedure with the final consonant in fan, man, ran (fann, mann, rann) until satisfied that the pupil understands the associations of sounds with symbols.

To test pupil proficiency and propensity in hearing initial sounds, medial sounds and final sounds, give the letter cards to the pupil:

Part I (initial items): f, m, n, r, s, v

Part II (vowels): a, e, i, o, u

Part III (final items): f, m, n, r, s, v

and tell him that you are going to say some words for him to spell with the letter cards. Say several real words to test his ability at this (fan, men, rim, sun, non). Now, test his ability to learn through the auditory mode by having him make *nonsense words.* Be sure to explain first that s/he is to make *nonsense* words from your sounds. Use: faf, mem, nin, ror, sus, maf, nam, vof, etc. When the pupil places the letter cards so that he correctly spells the nonsense words s/he should be complimented for the task. From this test it can be determined whether or not the pupil seems to have a special sensitivity for phonics (letter, symbols, sounds) and may very well learn best through this approach.

The final suggested auditory procedure is to have the pupil read nonsense words made by the investigator. Explain that he is to read what the letters say. Then arrange the cards to form other nonsense words, not of the same pattern as previously used. Try nonsense words such as: vum, saf, rem, niv, mon, fev, etc. making as many combinations as necessary to test this skill. Successful completion of these tasks as indicated probably shows that the pupil has a *phonics propensity* and can learn words best through this method.

The third and final test of the *VAM Test* series is to discover if the student learns best through a kinesthetic/tactile approach to teaching words. This approach combines all motor receptors and, as a result, is quite time consuming. Classroom teachers and reading teachers should plan to use this test only on those few students who seem to learn less efficiently through the visual and auditory modalities. This procedure requires a pupil to look at the word under discussion, visualize the position of the letters, pronounce the word, and write the word. After an elapse of 5-10 minutes, the pupil writes the word as a test of this propensity. Here is what to do.

Select several words unfamiliar to the pupil. These special words should vary in length from 6-7 to 10-11 letters. Use your own words or use these: vocabulary, similarity, importance, explanation, against, together, consider, etc. Show the child each word separately. Give him the flash card. Have him trace the letters after saying the word for him. As he traces the letters of the word he should say the word aloud.

He should then close his eyes and try to visualize the position of the letters as he says the word. Then he should be directed to open his eyes and look again at the flashcard to see if he was correct. He should say the word. If the pupil believes that he knows the word, remove the flashcard and have him write the word from memory. First, he should say the word, then he should visualize the letter order of structure, and finally he should write the word.

Then the word should be compared with the flash card. If the word is written correctly, this pupil may have a propensity for visual-motor kinesthesia and should learn words in this manner. If the pupil did not write the word correctly, repeat the procedure:

1. Show the word printed on the flashcard.

2. Pronounce the word for him.

3. Have him pronounce the word.

4. Give him the flashcard and have him trace the word.

5. He should say the word as he traces it.

6. Then he closes his eyes and visualizes the word.

7. He opens his eyes and looks again at the flashcard.

8. Then he says the word again.

9. If necessary, repeat these steps.

10. If successful, the pupil should write the word from memory.

11. As he writes, he says the word and visualizes the sequence.:
    a. say the word.
    b. visualize the serial arrangement.
    c. write the word.

12. The final step is to compare the pupil's response with the flashcard.

This then, is the *VAM Test.* From it you can learn how best to teach students the reading skills they need to know in order to read better. Teachers should plan lessons so that one or more of these learning modalities is emphasized. How to do that is explained in Chapter 9.

SUMMARY

The best place for teachers to start in helping students become better readers is to test them. Diagnose the reading problems and use that information to plan an effective reading instructional program.

There are four broad categories of tests for teachers to consider in the testing program. There are the formal, standardized, norm-referenced reading achievement tests and some of these are administered on a group (total class) basis while others are administered on an individual (one-to-one) basis. Then there are teacher-made informal tests called Informal Reading Inventories (IRI). Several excellent versions of these are available for teachers and the author's own Informal Diagnostic Reading Test is explained in this chapter. Also, that IDRT is printed in the appendix and teachers are urged to use it in the testing program. The third type of tests are the criterion- or objective-referenced tests which are based on the curriculum of the school. Students demonstrate their reading proficiency according to specific goals or criteria that have been established by the school and which are considered to be important. The performance of pupils is compared with the reference point of educational objectives rather than with normative performance of other students. The fourth type of test is that of modality strength or preference. There is evidence to indicate that some students learn best when lessons are presented in a visual manner. Others learn best when lessons are given in a manner that is auditory in nature and still other pupils learn best through motor processes. The problem facing the teacher, whether in the classroom or in the reading room, is the problem of testing students to discover how they learn best. Once this is known, appropriate therapy lessons can be constructed.

4
EVALUATION:
From Diagnosis to Prognosis

In the preceeding chapter reference was made to testing or diagnosis as the first step in any sound educational sequence. But testing by itself does little or nothing for the instructional program unless a penetrating evaluation of the test results is made by the teacher. That is to say, when the tests have been administered and scored, it remains for the teacher to evaluate them in terms of what they tell about pupil's reading deficiencies. Merely scoring tests is not enough. The teacher must look to what the results or information tells about pupil reading problems. This procedure is vital to the planning and organization of an instructional program that will fit the needs of the pupils for any sort of effective teaching effort.

It is imparative that the teacher adjust reading instruction to fit the pupils and this implies that s/he needs to know where the pupils are on the reading achievement continuum. The fundamental question to be asked at this juncture is, "What reading skills does this pupil need to know in order to become a better reader?" An examination and interpretation of the test scores will serve as a guide here and is the basis for the ensuing therapy.

STANDARDIZED, NORM-REFERENCED READING TESTS

As previously noted, these tests evaluate a student's performance on the basis of pre-established average reference points. The pupil may be above average, average, or below average in varying degrees along a continuum ranging from very high to very low. Usually this type of test is not used for diagnostic purposes but rather for comparisons with other students. Grade level scores in years and months are usually forthcoming for each subtest and a composite score is usually calculated and entered in the student's permanent record file.

Although this type of test is not very satisfactory for purposes of planning an instructional program, it does provide the teacher/diagnostician with some rough data which can be translated into broad guidelines. To illustrate this point, let us examine some ficticious data. Suppose you administered a reading test in which there were several subtests including 1) reading speed and accuracy, 2) vocabulary knowledge, and 3) a measure of comprehension. After you had scored all the tests, further suppose that you had results such as these in raw score form:

	Speed	Accuracy	Vocabulary	Comprehension
Tom	30	30	50	50
Sue	20	19	40	41
Bob	20	10	25	25
Mary	30	5	15	10
Steve	10	10	15	10

Our ficticious test has a maximum possible score as follows:

Speed = 35
Accuracy = 35
Vocabulary = 50
Comprehension = 50

These data tell us a great deal about student performance if we will take the time to examine them carefully. Usually this is not done. Usually teachers do not use this information for evaluative and diagnostic purposes, but it can be done as described below.

In evaluating the information available in this illustration, it would appear that Tom does not really seem to have any reading deficiencies, as shown on his performance for this test. Sue reads somewhat slower than Tom, can define fewer words, and appears to comprehend less well. But if we look at this more closely we will note that Sue is near to average in reading speed and is certainly quite accurate in her reading. Since our test is a timed test, that may be a factor in vocabulary and comprehension. Perhaps she read too slowly to finish all parts of the subtests. A recommendation for therapy should certainly include developing Sue's reading speed. A look at Bob's raw scores shows that accuracy suffers because he tried twenty speed paragraphs and had only half of them right. If he tried all 50 vocabulary items and had a score of 25 then he probably guessed at half of them and guessed wrong. The same for comprehension. A therapy program for Bob should include activities that develop reading accuracy, vocabulary knowledge, and comprehension skills because he obviously needs help in these areas.

Mary is even worse off. So much so that we can question whether or not she understood the directions of the test and/or what was expected of her. Either that or she is a severely retarded reader. Scoring five out of thirty in accuracy could occur by chance. Fifteen words out of 50 on the vocabulary test could show that perhaps, she knows a few of the very simple or easy words and guessed at the remainder. The same conclusions could be made on the comprehension test. So it is important for the teacher to look at the responses on the test booklet or separate answer sheet and define the pattern of errors. If there appears to be a hit-and-miss correct response, then we can assume that the student was guessing at the answers. If the pattern is such that the responses are correct in the beginning of each subtest and falls off sharply thereafter, then we can assume that the student probably knew the easier material and soon arrived at his/her frustration level. So you will want to carefully study the specific responses made by the students and then decide upon the pattern of error shown. Afterwards, you can decide what was going on in the student's mind as s/he responded to the test.

Steve seems to fare better than either Bob or Mary because his problem seems to be limited to poor reading speed. He tried ten and had all of them correct so his accuracy is excellent. He is just a slow reader. But that can be rather easily remedied. Then his limited responses in the vocabulary section could also be a result of slow speed. Again, look to the test booklet and see what the pattern is. Did he attempt the first fifteen and not the rest? If so, this is an excellent indication of his slowness in reading. Do the same for comprehension and see what conclusions you can draw from those responses.

Admittedly the evaluation just described is crude and the classroom teacher/reading teacher would want to know more of the specifics regarding each problem reader's reading problem. The best way to do this is to sit down with each student and discuss his/her test performance on an individual basis. Have the test booklet and/or answer sheet for each one available and examine the performance in this one-to-one setting. Show the student where the errors are and find out why they were made. Ask him/her if s/he was guessing, if directions were not clear, if the test was too threatening, etc. The reader's responses will give the teacher/therapist considerable insight into organizing and planning a program of correction.

INFORMAL TESTS

Evaluating the other categories of tests noted in Chapter 3 is a relatively simple task. Usually, an effective therapy program can be structured on the basis of a direct readout of pupil responses. This is similar to the procedure suggested above in using standardized norm-referenced reading tests and with informal tests the job of doing this is rather easy. The fundamental consideration is to again look at the specific skill strengths and weaknesses of individual student performance, look at the pattern of errors or mistakes, and look to the percent of achievement.

By this time it should be obvious to the reader that our concern here is not so much for average grade-level expectations but for each student's performance as an individual. Regardless of where your students are in your classroom or in your special reading room, you should be less concerned with the grade level of attainment and more concerned with the student as a person. If you do this, it means that you will look to each student as having individual strengths and weaknesses and you will downgrade the consideration that students should be brought up to grade level.

Although it is true that some students in any classroom or group have reading problems similar to others in that same classroom or group, generally the reading profiles of achievement vary widely. It is on the basis of the Reading Achievement Profile (the Reading Profile At-A-Glance) that teachers and therapists should concentrate because it is on that profile that the reading therapy program is based.

Regardless of the kind of informal tests you administer to your students, you will find the results easy to evaluate or interpret. That is to say, teach students according to the problem skill areas as indicated by low performance scores. If a score is low, we can assume that 1) the student is deficient in that skill, or 2) s/he did not understand what was required. A brief individual conference can clear up these points and the teacher/therapist can continue accordingly.

If a student is deficient in a particular reading skill or cluster of skills, then that is the place for therapy or correction to begin. Again, this is where a direct readout can be used to guide the learning program.

If a student did not understand what was expected in the test situation, then it would be wise for the teacher/therapist to give an alternate form of the test to the student and again test to determine where the reading problems are.

In evaluating the Reading Profile-At-A-Glance the teacher/therapist can see where the student's weak areas are and plan to remedy them. To clarify this point, let us examine the profiles of our ficticious students noted in the first part of this chapter. We can study Tom, Sue, Bob, Mary and Steve and come to some precise conclusions for proceeding with an effective therapy program.

As previously noted, Tom is an excellent reader as indicated by his performance on the standardized, norm-referenced reading achievement test. He reads rapidly and with excellent accuracy. His vocabulary is very high and so is his comprehension. Because of this, the classroom teacher should not be concerned with further testing. It would serve no real purpose. This student is reading exceptionally well so let him continue reading in an individualized reading program and then periodically discuss with you the books he has read

However, if you did decide to test Tom with the Informal Diagnostic Reading Tests, the results of his performance would closely parallel the performance noted in Figure 4.1. All subtest scores are perfect except for number 13, phonetic spelling and numbers 24 and 25, clozure V and VI. Here Tom missed one each and this is certainly nothing to be concerned about. So the suggestion that Tom continue in his individualized reading program is valid as noted.

The same, or nearly the same could be said for Sue. She is another good reader, but she may read less rapidly than Tom. You may wish to concentrate on speed improvement and test her again later on. You could administer the Informal Diagnostic Reading Tests to her and perhaps learn about an important reading deficiency. Figure 4.2 shows her performance. Examining her Profile-At-A-Glance it is readily apparent that syllabication and phonetic spelling appear to be less well understood than are the majority of the skills. Also, Sue

DIAGNOSIS
Informal Diagnostic Reading Tests for Teachers

Student's name _____ *Tom* _____ Date ___ *9/30* ___
Grade __*4*__ Sex __*M*__ IQ _*135*_ CA _*10-2*_ Birthdate ___ *7/30* ___
Teacher's name ___ *Mrs. Able* ___ School ___ *Alpha* ___

Subtests	Raw Score	Profile-At-A-Glance
		0 · · · · 25 · · · · 50 · · · · 75 · · 100
1. Visual I (ooo⚠o)	4/4	
2. Visual II (bbmbb)	4/4	
3. Visual III (hbhhh)	4/4	
4. Alphabet I (sequence)	26/26	
5. Alphabet II (f, , ,)	4/4	
6. Alphabet III (, k,)	4/4	
7. Auditory I (Initial Consonants)	4/4	
8. Aud. II (Final Consonants)	4/4	
9. Aud. III (Initial Cons. Blends)	4/4	
10. Aud. IV (Initial Cons. Digraphs)	4/4	
11. Aud. V (Phonograms)	4/4	
12. Aud. VI (Syllabication)	4/4	
13. Aud-Vis. I (Phonetic Spelling)	7/8	
14. Aud-Vis. II (Long Vowel Sounds)	5/5	
15. Aud-Vis III (Short Vowel Sounds)	5/5	
16. Aud-Vis. IV (Pref.-Roots-Suff.)	10/10	
17. Letter b position	4/4	
18. Basic Sight Test I	100/100	
19. Basic Sight Test II	100/100	
20. CLOZURE I	15/15	
21. CLOZURE II	15/15	
22. CLOZURE III	15/15	
23. CLOZURE IV	15/15	
24. CLOZURE V	14/15	
25. CLOZURE VI	14/15	

Summary of Observations:

Note: This form may be reproduced for teacher classroom use.

Figure 4.1

missed two words on the prefix-root-suffix subtest. So it would seem that she could benefit from some minimal instruction in these areas. Then, looking to her clozure responses, it looks like she is reaching toward her maximum performance at level six. So the Informal Diagnostic Reading Tests tend to substantiate the results of the standardized test and we can conclude that both tests are valid for Sue and she is performing at a better than average level.

Therapy for Sue should include reading activities to increase her reading speed, activities to help her with the syllabication of words, and more practice in spelling the sounds she hears. But she should not be pressured because she is doing well and after a therapy period of a few months she should be retested. Chances are she will have made some improvement, but not too much because she really does not have that far to go.

Bob's standardized test results show that he needs to work on accuracy as well as vocabulary and comprehension. His Profile-At-A-Glance is shown in Figure 4.3. From the Profile it is easy to understand his reading problems. His knowledge of phonograms, although acceptable is a skill which could be strengthened. He should definitely receive instruction in syllabication skills and in sound-symbol relationships with more nonsense words. You may want to hold off on the long and short vowel sounds for a little while and concentrate on prefixes-roots-suffixes instead. Also, his knowledge of the basic sight vocabulary needs to be strengthened and his reading for comprehension should be improved. His relatively poor showing on the standardized reading test is explained quite well through his performance on the Informal Diagnostic Reading Tests. No doubt he guessed on many of the speed paragraphs, the vocabulary, and on comprehension paragraphs. The reasons for this are apparent from the Profile. He is weak in syllabication skills and the higher level sound-symbol relationships as brought out by the subtest on phonetic spelling. He has difficulty with roots and affixes so many multisyllabic words are too much for him.

DIAGNOSIS
Informal Diagnostic Reading Tests for Teachers

Student's name _____ *Sue* _____ Date ___ *10/20* ___
Grade __*4*__ Sex __*F*__ IQ _*120*_ CA _*10-4*_ Birthdate ___ *6/20* ___
Teacher's name _____ *Mrs. Able* _____ School ___ *Alpha* ___

Subtests	Raw Score	Profile-At-A-Glance
		0····25····50····75··100
1. Visual I (ooo▲o)	4/4	
2. Visual II (bbmbb)	4/4	
3. Visual III (hbhhh)	4/4	
4. Alphabet I (sequence)	26/26	
5. Alphabet II (f, , ,)	4/4	
6. Alphabet III (, k,)	4/4	
7. Auditory I (Initial Consonants)	4/4	
8. Aud. II (Final Consonants)	4/4	
9. Aud. III (Initial Cons. Blends)	4/4	
10. Aud. IV (Initial Cons. Digraphs)	4/4	
11. Aud. V (Phonograms)	4/4	
12. Aud. VI (Syllabication)	3/4	
13. Aud-Vis. I (Phonetic Spelling)	6/8	
14. Aud-Vis. II (Long Vowel Sounds)	5/5	
15. Aud-Vis III (Short Vowel Sounds)	5/5	
16. Aud-Vis. IV (Pref.-Roots-Suff.)	8/10	
17. Letter b position	4/4	
18. Basic Sight Test I	100/100	
19. Basic Sight Test II	99/100	
20. CLOZURE I	15/15	
21. CLOZURE II	15/15	
22. CLOZURE III	15/15	
23. CLOZURE IV	15/15	
24. CLOZURE V	14/15	
25. CLOZURE VI	13/15	

Summary of Observations:

Note: This form may be reproduced for teacher classroom use.

Figure 4.2

Another enlightening discovery in Bob's profile is in the basic sight vocabulary and clozure stories. He apparently does not comprehend more because he lacks a knowledge of certain basic words and is unable to read beyond a given level because of that. Work on the basic sight vocabulary is another element to include in the therapy sessions for Bob. He also needs to read relatively simple material for comprehension. Stories which are of a lower than fourth grade readability difficulty, perhaps third grade, would benefit him in helping him comprehend better.

An examination of Mary's Profile page in the Informal Diagnostic Reading Tests will show the major reason why she is not performing well. Her potential for achievement is limited and this is indicated by her somewhat low I.Q. score. In some ways she is doing about as well as could be expected if we think of her as a person and are not thinking of grade level expectations. The standardized reading test shows her to be deficient in accuracy as well as speed because the speed score is probably spurious. Her knowledge of vocabulary is quite limited and, as a result, her comprehension suffers.

Mary's Profile-At-A-Glance shows visual perception to be excellent as is her knowledge of the alphabet, except for subtest 6 where she was required to indicate which letters came before and after a given letter. Yet this subskill and the others through subtest 10 show her performance usage and her syllabication skills need strengthening. Here is where a study helper could be of great value.

Mary's knowledge of how to spell the sounds of English as shown by subtest 13 is greatly limited so the teacher should plan appropriate exercises with her. Then, once Mary has begun to understand this process, the use of a study helper is the next step in her therapy program. The same would be true for subtest 16, roots and affixes.

Sight vocabulary for Mary is another part of the therapy program for us to consider. She needs to know the basic words before she can hope to master more difficult words. And her limited knowledge of sight words probably accounts for the poor showing on the clozure

DIAGNOSIS
Informal Diagnostic Reading Tests for Teachers

Student's name _____ *Bob* _____ Date ___ *10/10* ___
Grade _*4*_ Sex _*M*_ IQ _*101*_ CA _*10-0*_ Birthdate ___ *10/10* ___
Teacher's name ____ *Mrs. Able* ____ School ____ *Alpha* ____

Subtests	Raw Score	Profile-At-A-Glance 0····25····50····75··100			
1. Visual I (ooo△o)	4/4				
2. Visual II (bbmbb)	4/4				
3. Visual III (hbhhh)	4/4				
4. Alphabet I (sequence)	26/26				
5. Alphabet II (f, , ,)	4/4				
6. Alphabet III (, k,)	4/4				
7. Auditory I (Initial Consonants)	4/4				
8. Aud. II (Final Consonants)	4/4				
9. Aud. III (Initial Cons. Blends)	4/4				
10. Aud. IV (Initial Cons. Digraphs)	4/4				
11. Aud. V (Phonograms)	3/4				
12. Aud. VI (Syllabication)	2/4				
13. Aud-Vis. I (Phonetic Spelling)	4/8				
14. Aud-Vis. II (Long Vowel Sounds)	4/5				
15. Aud-Vis III (Short Vowel Sounds)	4/5				
16. Aud-Vis. IV (Pref.-Roots-Suff.)	5/10				
17. Letter b position	4/4				
18. Basic Sight Test I	80/100				
19. Basic Sight Test II	70/100				
20. CLOZURE I	15/15				
21. CLOZURE II	14/15				
22. CLOZURE III	13/15				
23. CLOZURE IV	10/15				
24. CLOZURE V	—				
25. CLOZURE VI	—				

Summary of Observations:

Note: This form may be reproduced for teacher classroom use.

Figure 4.3

passages. Mary did well on the first one; about average on level II, and not well at all on level III. For the present, then, she seems to be able to read acceptably at a second grade level and this is not bad for someone with limited potential who is actually in the fourth grade.

Mary should continue receiving help from the teacher and others in the classroom. She can benefit from appropriate practice and therapy as noted, but for now teacher expectations should not be too high. If they are, and Mary fails to achieve then her self-image can be severely damaged. For Mary, realistic expectations are the best guide for the teacher. Grade level expectations are out of the question and should not be considered.

Our final illustration is Steve, who performed well for a slow reader. His accuracy was excellent on the standardized test. His vocabulary and comprehension scores were low and an examination of his responses showed why. Every item he attempted was correct. So we can conclude that he is an extremely slow reader. His performance on the Informal Diagnostic Reading Tests supports this. All subtests were well done until he reached number 24. Then, because of the inordinate amount of time he took for the entire test, it was evident that he was too tired to continue doing well. Subtest 25 was beyond his capabilities. So Steve is able to read at a level of difficulty which corresponds to his potential, but he is extremely slow. He may be a syllable-by-syllable or letter-by-letter reader and needs to learn to speed up. He may have had too much phonic analysis in the beginning stages of reading instruction and simply continues to examine each word accordingly. He needs to be taught to read faster and mechanical devices for increasing his speed should be included in the therapy program. It seems that flash cards are a must for Steve and the therapist could begin with single words, then go on to two word phrases and later to three word phrases. The tachistoscope would also help and so would a controlled reader device. Steve needs to be made to read rapidly until he can do so on his own and without the aid of instruments. It may take a considerable amount of time, so

DIAGNOSIS
Informal Diagnostic Reading Tests for Teachers

Student's name _____ *Mary* _____ Date ___ *10/12* ___

Grade ___ Sex _*F*_ IQ _*80*_ CA _*10-2*_ Birthdate ___ *10/5* ___

Teacher's name _____ *Mrs. Able* _____ School ___ *Alpha* ___

Subtests	Raw Score	Profile-At-A-Glance
		0····25····50····75··100
1. Visual I (oooΔo)	4/4	
2. Visual II (bbmbb)	4/4	
3. Visual III (hbhhh)	4/4	
4. Alphabet I (sequence)	26/26	
5. Alphabet II (f, , ,)	4/4	
6. Alphabet III (, k,)	3/4	
7. Auditory I (Initial Consonants)	3/4	
8. Aud. II (Final Consonants)	3/4	
9. Aud. III (Initial Cons. Blends)	3/4	
10. Aud. IV (Initial Cons. Digraphs)	3/4	
11. Aud. V (Phonograms)	2/4	
12. Aud. VI (Syllabication)	2/4	
13. Aud-Vis. I (Phonetic Spelling)	2/8	
14. Aud-Vis. II (Long Vowel Sounds)	5/5	
15. Aud-Vis III (Short Vowel Sounds)	5/5	
16. Aud-Vis. IV (Pref.-Roots-Suff.)	4/10	
17. Letter b position	4/4	
18. Basic Sight Test I	75/100	
19. Basic Sight Test II	60/100	
20. CLOZURE I	14/15	
21. CLOZURE II	12/15	
22. CLOZURE III	5/15	
23. CLOZURE IV	—	
24. CLOZURE V	—	
25. CLOZURE VI	—	

Summary of Observations:

Note: This form may be reproduced for teacher classroom use.

Figure 4.4

neither Steve nor the therapist should be discouraged if there is little or no immediate improvement.

SUMMARY

In this chapter, the procedures involved in evaluation were noted. Fictitious scores on a standardized test were interpreted in a diagnostic fashion to illustrate how this could be done. Then comparisons with fictitious scores on the Informal Diagnostic Reading Tests were made.

Evaluation can be simple or difficult depending on the nature of the performer and his/her performance on tests. There is nothing esoteric about evaluation as noted in this chapter and common sense here is one of the therapist's best guides. In the next chapter, some ideas will be presented which will help the teacher prepare for therapy. This, too, is a vital step for all to consider.

DIAGNOSIS
Informal Diagnostic Reading Tests for Teachers

Student's name _____ *Steve* _____ Date ___ *10/13* ___

Grade __*4*__ Sex __*M*__ IQ __*97*__ CA __*10-6*__ Birthdate ___ — ___

Teacher's name _____ *Mrs. Able* _____ School _____ *Alpha* _____

Subtests	Raw Score	Profile-At-A-Glance
		0 · · · · 25 · · · · 50 · · · · 75 · · 100
1. Visual I (ooo▲o)	4/4	
2. Visual II (bbmbb)	4/4	
3. Visual III (hbhhh)	4/4	
4. Alphabet I (sequence)	26/26	
5. Alphabet II (f, , ,)	4/4	
6. Alphabet III (, k,)	4/4	
7. Auditory I (Initial Consonants)	4/4	
8. Aud. II (Final Consonants)	4/4	
9. Aud. III (Initial Cons. Blends)	4/4	
10. Aud. IV (Initial Cons. Digraphs)	4/4	
11. Aud. V (Phonograms)	4/4	
12. Aud. VI (Syllabication)	4/4	
13. Aud-Vis. I (Phonetic Spelling)	7/8	
14. Aud-Vis. II (Long Vowel Sounds)	5/5	
15. Aud-Vis III (Short Vowel Sounds)	5/5	
16. Aud-Vis. IV (Pref.-Roots-Suff.)	9/10	
17. Letter b position	4/4	
18. Basic Sight Test I	100/100	
19. Basic Sight Test II	99/100	
20. CLOZURE I	15/15	
21. CLOZURE II	15/15	
22. CLOZURE III	14/15	
23. CLOZURE IV	14/15	
24. CLOZURE V	10/15	
25. CLOZURE VI	5/15	

Summary of Observations:

Note: This form may be reproduced for teacher classroom use.

Figure 4.5

5
ANTICIPATION:
A Prelude to Therapy

The effective perceptive, creative teacher is one who has the ability to view a classroom learning situation from several positions. Two of the most important ways to perceive the class or group, or teaching procedure are 1) as a macrostructure, or global concept (the *forest*, if you will), and 2) as a microstructure or small, individual elements (the *trees*, for example). In viewing the macrostructure of the teaching/learning process, the classroom/reading teacher will look to the broad, all-inclusive environment/climate as a whole. In the microstructure, the teacher/therapist will view the individual elements, the segments or integral parts of the total process which composes or makes up the entire learning environment. Both viewpoints are crucial to effective teaching and learning in the reading therapy process.

MACROSTRUCTURE

In order to help you think in terms of the broad, global aspects (the *forest*) of your present position, look to the forces that impinge on you; the forces that effect what you do. Indeed there are many of them to consider and all exert an influence to some degree. This total cluster of factors operating together in some synchronized fashion is the macrostructure for us to note: the reading taxonomy.

MICROSTRUCTURE

This refers to each individual factor which composes or makes up the total teaching/learning environment, the macrostructure, in which we find ourselves. There are so many of them that it is just about impossible to list them all so let us consider only a few, each of which can in turn become a macrostructure.

A vital part of the macrostructure is the community where you teach. It, in turn, is composed of many factors and forces which exert an influence (for good or ill) and all of them need to be considered when you plan and organize your teaching efforts.

The school itself is another vital factor in the macrostructure and it has a number of dimensions. Although it is classified as a microstructure for our purposes here, it can also be view as a macrostructure because of the component parts going into it. So each macrostructure has its own microstructure on down to the smallest of elements in the educational scheme, the letters of the alphabet.

BASIC TASKS

Each teacher has the responsibility of synthesizing the macro/micro structures so that they form a viable time line which is then used as a guide to instruction. Whether it is the teacher in the self-contained classroom, departmentalized classroom, or open classroom there is the major task of anticipating needs. And this is also true for the reading teacher who works with students in the reading room.

Anticipation of needs is a preplanning and preorganizational step requiring the teacher to formulate a mental image, a construct, of what will be needed in order to make the teaching/learning activity or activities effective for all students. Anticipation is a step in which the teacher pauses to look ahead (in anticipation) and conceptualize what will happen under ideal circumstances and also to think of what could happen as alternatives to that ideal, just in case.

The basic tasks of anticipation involve the goal of instruction as the reference point. This is why it is so important to test students as previously noted because the tests provide the goal(s). Once the goal has been determined the teacher can work backwards to the first instructional session or meeting with the student.

Anticipation is concerned with many factors so it can be classified as a macrostructure and it works like this:

Goals or Objectives = Improving comprehension skills

When = By the end of three (4 - 5?) weeks

How (medium) = Special clozure lessons +

For whom = Mary X

Micro factors = Collect appropriate materials to include: special clozure pages, response sheet, pencil, commercially prepared comp. ex. vocab. cards+

Plan with Mary (individual conference) what she is to do. Organize the class so the plans can be carried out and this will include 1) explaining to other students what is going to happen, 2) supplying them with appropriate meaningful activities.

Another way of looking at the process of anticipation is to think in terms of a *time-line*. Many teachers do this more or less automatically. Others, if they do it at all it is with great difficulty. Actually, it takes a special kind of person to be able to conceptualize the framework of a time-line and then to follow through with it. But then good teachers are a special kind of person.

DISCUSSION

Although it is not possible to explain the concept of anticipation in specific detail for each and every learning experience teachers and students will complete, there are some broad considerations to note. One of these is concerned with the materials or supplies needed by students. These should be readily available for immediate use when the students reach this point in the lesson or experience. Another guideline has to do with the learning aids which will be used by the teacher. These include items such as films, film strips, charts, audio/ visual tapes, transparancies, etc. Teachers should preview all films, video tapes, etc. which are used as instructional aids so that there is a prior knowledge of their content. Furthermore, it is usually necessary to make notes as to what the material is all about so that the students can be prepared for viewing the film or whatever.

When teachers properly, anticipate instruction procedures, they may discover that a large chart is needed to help explain ideas, or a transparancy on the overhead projector could be used to great advantage. Therefore, it will be necessary to prepare ahead of time such instructional aids as warranted.

The physical setting is another broad consideration which includes a number of subfactors. The physical plant can be thought of as a macrostructure or macroclimate made up of components which include temperature in the classroom, humidity, space, lighting, acoustics, and so on. The teacher must also look ahead and try to anticipate whether or not the physical setting is adequate. Perhaps learning would be more effective if the class or group, or individual moved to a different room or area. A very good illustration of this need can be made by thinking of the language experience approach to reading. Frequently students and teacher make a trip into the community so they can have the first-hand sensory experiences involved in learning certain concepts. In this instance the classroom environment is not enough so the students go elsewhere. Now, when this happens or actually before this happens, the teacher must anticipate several things. Will school busses be used? If so, this will necessitate proper scheduling. Will students be away from school all day? If so, they will have to eat and appropriate arrangements will need to be made. And so on through the many details that are so vital to effective student learning.

Another broad consideration teachers need to note is the cluster of factors which go to make up the sound rationale for a lesson. As we will see in the next chapter, it is necessary for teachers to know not only what the students will be doing, but also why they will be doing it. This means that teachers should prepare themselves to explain to students why they are doing what they are doing; explain how the learning activity will benefit them as students; tell why it is necessary for them to spend their time doing what they are doing. Only in this way will the educational experience reach its full learning potential.

ILLUSTRATION

All too frequently the typical classroom teacher has not been trained adequately in coping with the need to anticipate all the requirements of learning experiences. As was noted in Chapter 1 the fault rests with institutions of higher learning, the colleges and universities engaged in teacher education. This means that teachers usually have to pick up the anticipation process on their own.

In order to help fill in what could be a blank area in a teacher's education, let us closely examine the following Time-Line Macro-structure and evaluate the ensuing microstructure evolving from it. It seems best to use a relatively simple illustration here so we will not become overwhelmed by detail. This example is one of many ways to illustrate the idea of and need for anticipating procedures and needs. So teachers should not think that this is the only way to do it.

Let us imagine that you are a teacher in a classroom and you want to work with Bob (Chapter 4). He is the student who was given a reading test and his performance indicated that he needed help in speed-accuracy-vocabulary comprehension. The goal which Bob's teacher should set is that of helping him improve in all four reading skill clusters. To do this effectively, the teacher could anticipate needs, materials, and procedures somewhat as follows:

- Think of meeting with Bob individually for 20 minutes.

- Think of what the other class members should be doing and structure their activities so no one will need your help until later.

The teacher will want to explain the program to the class as a whole before having the smaller groups meet and before meeting with Bob. For Tom's group it will be necessary to check and see if more trade or library books are needed. This is something Tom could do and then relay the information to the teacher. Respond accordingly. If more books are needed, but not available, have students go on to the alternate plan which would include reading in the other subject areas. If social studies reports are to be made, students could prepare them at this point. If science demonstrations are to be given, students could quietly work on them now.

The students in Sue's group could go to the darkened area of the classroom to use the controlled reader. The teacher should make sure that the correct filmstrip has been placed in the projector and that worksheets for that exercise are available. It then remains to be decided who will check the worksheet responses and how the checking will be done. After that, the group should have meaningful work scheduled in the event they finish the filmstrip before the teacher concludes the individual work with Bob.

With Steve's group there should also be no problem. Members of the group can work quietly in pairs and use the small, hand-held type tachistoscope as well as flash cards. They can help each other until they sense that they have had enough drill. Then they could go on to read material such as the *Readers Digest Reading Skill Builders* or the *Webster New Practice Readers* or material from the *S.R.A. Reading Improvement Kit,* etc. With these activities, the students can help themselves improve their reading speed and vocabulary knowledge as well as comprehension. Appropriate arrangements for checking any activities could be made as agreed to by all concerned. The teacher should anticipate that some students may need help and one or two pupils should be assigned to that task. (See Chapter 7 for more about study helpers.)

When we come to Mary's group, we have similar learning activities to consider. They, too, need to improve the same reading skills as the members of Steve's group, but here the level or content is different. Words that are very easy to recognize should be used with these students. Special types of activities to develop comprehension skills should be used and the teacher will need to provide them. Also, a means of checking student responses should be planned by all concerned.

Although the anticipation of student and material needs appears to be involved and a long-drawn out or extended dialogue is needed to explain to students what will happen, in actuality it takes only a few minutes of student and teacher time. Then it is a matter of letting the pupils get down to work while the teacher turns attention to Bob.

In working with Bob on an individual basis, the teacher or the therapist should have Bob's test results available so that these can be used as the basis for instruction as noted in the previous chapter. A quick check of Bob's responses will remind him of what skills he needs to work on and the lesson can proceed accordingly.

The teacher, having anticipated the words Bob needs to learn, will have already prepared vocabulary flash cards. Both can sit down together and riffle through the cards; the teacher can flash them and Bob can quickly (and quietly) call them out. Or the small, hand-held tachistoscope can be used for this same purpose and Bob's responses can be recorded on tape. Afterwards, he can play back the tape and check the accuracy of his responses.

As a second phase to developing reading speed and accuracy the teacher could use any of the many tracking activities available for these purposes. Students usually enjoy the challenge of such material so the activity can be enjoyable.

To increase Bob's comprehension skills, the teacher may choose to use appropriate material such as the *Reader's Digest Reading Skill Builders, Webster New Practice Readers, S.R.A. Learning Laboratory* materials, *California Programmed Reading Booklets,* etc. Teachers and therapists should check the Appendices for a comprehensive list of available commercially prepared materials.

The final step in Bob's lesson could very well be some drill in word attack skills. Again the teacher/therapist will want to refer to Bob's test results to find out where he is deficient. Remind him of this and then provide appropriate learning materials to overcome the problem.

As you can readily see, there is nothing special about the therapy program. Good teachers have been doing theses things for years and doing them with excellent results. But it does take some special type of abilities on the part of the teacher. One ability is to anticipate what is to be done for each student or group. Another ability is to place some trust in all class members, trust them to do what they are supposed to do after the teacher has adequately explained everything to them. Then there is the ability to let go. Not all teachers feel comfortable when the students in their classes are doing different things

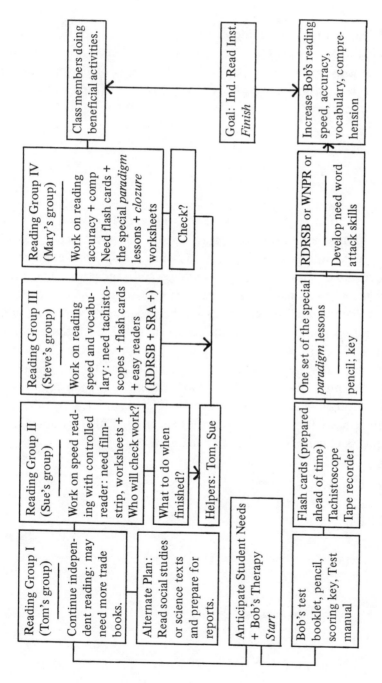

Figure 5.1: Anticipation: The Time Line Macro/Micro Structure

at the same time. Furthermore, not every teacher can handle what might be called an instructional juggling act as outlined above. But, as has already been noted, it takes a special type of person to be an effective teacher and the process of anticipation is representative of only one such ability.

SUMMARY

Anticipation is the process of looking ahead to what will take place during instructional sessions. To do this the teacher should form a careful mental picture of the entire scope and content of what will take place (the macrostructure) and prepare all concerned for what will take place. It is then necessary to anticipate the needs of all students, thinking in terms of the procedures, materials, and other related items (the microstructure) that will make the learning experience successful.

These points are discussed in this chapter and their use is illustrated for you to consider. This represents one way to intrepret and follow through with the concept. In the next chapter, you will read about the need for and importance of planning. This is another crucial process in helping all students read better.

6
PLANNING:
The Key to Effective Therapy

If there is one skill or ability which sets the effective teacher apart from those who are less than effective it is the talent for planning. This capability for developing a viable teaching scheme so that all students will learn to their maximum potential is the hallmark of what teaching is all about. Planning is so vital to any teaching/learning endeavor that teachers are given books in which to set down their plans for each day and each week. Furthermore, teachers are frequently given free time during the day, time which is to be devoted to planning the educational activities for students.

It is, no doubt, obvious to the reader that there are strengths and weakenesses to planning and no one instructional design is going to adequately fit all teachers, classrooms, or reading rooms. This is too much to expect. But there are some vital areas or ideas to consider when planning the learning activities of students and these will be presented in this chapter.

A major strength of planning is that it provides the teacher with a map to follow and so it can be considered a guide to be used in the

---

This originally appeared in *Education*, September-October, 1969 and is reprinted with permission.

education of students. But a guide is just that and no more. And it is probably here that teachers become fearful of planning. They may believe that planning inhibits their creativity, but this is simply untrue. Actually proper planning enhances the opportunity for creative teaching as we shall see below. Plans are made to be followed up to a point and then adapted as the learning situation warrants. So teachers should not be afraid to plan because changes can be made.

There are several dimensions to planning effective reading and language instruction for students at all age grade levels and special subject matter areas. One dimension is overplanning. Teachers are cautioned against this because it can indeed be detrimental to the learning environment. The same can be said for underplanning. So the goal for teachers to achieve is that of optimum planning which is done for the benefit of the class as a whole, the various groups within the class, and the individual students.

Before we go into a detailed discussion of planning educational activities for students, let us first consider one major objection which teachers raise against it. This is the assumption that teaching is an art and therefore, cannot be bound, stapled, or mutilated. Parameters cannot be drawn for an artistic work because none exist. Art, like beauty, is in the eye of the beholder. Without doubt, this is a true statement and one to be cherished. Artistry in teaching is the goal toward which all of us as educators are striving. But few of us are truely gifted enough to provide our pupils with such artistry day after day. Moreover, I would not presume to teach such artistry because it must come from each individual teacher in each classroom throughout the land.

Since the art of teaching cannot be taught, I want to do the next best thing and that is to provide a viable plan for teaching, a plan so serviceable that it will allow teachers freedom to become artists. This plan has as its focus the craft of teaching and craft is essential to any artistic endeavor. No one can honestly deny the idea that the artist who paints must master the craft of painting before s/he can aspire to true art, nor can anyone honestly deny the idea that the photographer who seeks to be an artist in that medium must first of all master the mechanics of the camera as well as the properties of the film. And this is just the beginning.

So craft is essential to the artist. Craft is also essential to the teacher. There are seven steps for teachers to master as the craft factors in effective teaching; seven steps to meaningful educational experiences for students.

The following suggestions, although comprehensive in scope, should not be thought of as the only end to which teachers should strive, but rather as a beginning that will ultimately lead to the goal of more effective pupil education. It is not enough for the teacher to merely follow these procedures in a mechanical manner. Although that would be more conducive to pupil learning than many present-day classroom practices, the best use would be as a reference point or base for the teacher's own subsequent unique artful methodology.

ORIENTATION

In planning any skill-building lesson or experience for pupils, the teacher should include several basic factors, each of which is pertinent to the total learning endeavor. One of the first considerations is *purpose.* The teacher should ask him/herself about the purpose or purposes of the proposed lesson and what s/he expects to accomplish with the pupils. It is necessary to have these purposes in mind so that they may be used as guides during the lesson and as one method of evaluation after the lesson has been completed.

A second major consideration has to do with *procedures.* The teacher needs to know how s/he will proceed in executing the lesson. S/he should think through the problem of sequence and ask him/herself if s/he really knows how s/he will go about presenting the lesson to the pupils. S/He should know not only what s/he is going to do, but how it will be done.

The third and final initial consideration has to do with the fact that the lesson or experience must be *meaningful* to those who are learning. Therefore, the teacher must constantly ask him/herself whether the lesson or experience has meaning for pupils. This concept does *not* ask whether they like the work or want to participate in it. If the teacher moves too far in this direction s/he is in danger of humoring children and submitting to their whims of the moment. In modern education, this leaves much to be desired. Rather, the teacher should ask if the lesson has meaning for the child in this context: Does the lesson make sense? Does each one in the group understand the nature and importance of the lesson for him/herself as a learner? Does each pupil realize the necessity for spending time on the lesson or activity?

If properly approached by the teacher, lessons and other school activities can have such vital meaning to most pupils that they will usually enter into them with eager anticipation. To achieve this end the teacher must set the stage for learning and subsequent participation. S/He should assist pupils in realizing the values of the activities to be carried out. The suggested sequence is noted below.

THE SEVEN STEPS

In order for the teacher to properly achieve the desired results in learning, to assure augmentation of the purposes, to solidify the procedures, and to make the activity meaningful to all (or almost all) pupils, the following steps are proffered. Each activity in which teachers and pupils participate should be guided by this sequence:

1. Introduction and aims.
2. Familiarization with lesson.

3. Demonstration of procedures.

4. Initial questions by students.

5. Participation by students.

6. Evaluation of exercise.

7. Final questioning by students.

Why these particular seven steps? Why these special procedures for each lesson? Let us take each of them individually and determine why it is important.

Introduction

Here the teacher introduces the work to be accomplished. At this point s/he sets the stage for learning. This is where background information is provided so that pupils are not plunged immediately into the task. Instead, the teacher speaks to the students and phrases the statements so that pupil attention is directed toward what is to be accomplished. A part of the introduction will be devoted to an explanation of the importance of the lesson for the pupil as a learner. It is the teacher's task to explain why the work is necessary, how it will help the pupils, and relate that which is unknown to that already known. When this step is properly carried out, it will aid students in understanding the value of the lesson for them as individual learners. It will help them because their attention is focused on the activity instead of somewhere else. Furthermore, it will help make the lesson meaningful to them because they understand the need for the work. The introduction is the first crucial step in the craft of teaching.

Familiarization

Here the teacher and pupils skim over the lesson together and they can see the scope of the material. The teacher provides time for them to examine the work so that it is not strange to them. If children are allowed sufficient time to glance over the work assigned, they will have some indication of the nature and content of the task. This step has the advantage of augmenting the meaningful aspect of the lesson and helping pupils realize its value. Furthermore, the teacher has the opportunity to point out the relationship between the present activity and past understandings. Moreover, the teacher should observe how well the children utilize the skills involved in skimming. The familiarization step is the second crucial craft factor.

Demonstration

In this step the teacher should work out one or two examples to illustrate how the learning task is to be done. The teacher actually shows pupils how to do it. This step has the advantage of helping them more clearly grasp those concepts which may have been nebulous. Ordinarily, two or three illustrations should be sufficient and, if most pupils seem to understand what is expected, the teacher can proceed to the next step. If, however, it is evident that most of them do not understand what is expected, more teaching in the form of demonstration is necessary. If all but a few appear to understand what they are to do, the teacher should plan to continue with the next step, but indicate to those who do not understand that further explanation will be forthcoming as soon as the teacher is free to do so. Demonstration is the vital third craft factor.

Initial Questioning

At the conclusion of the demonstration step, pupils should be given time to ask questions about the lesson. This is *not* a teacher-questioning period but a time for the students to clarify their conceptions or misconceptions. The advantage of this step is such that it serves as an additional check indicating how well the teacher has communicated with the children. If there are too many questions, the teacher has not explained as coherently as desired or the relationship between the known and the unknown has not been as clearly noted as the teacher thought it was. Another inherent advantage to this step is the increased rapport generated by the teacher's acceptance of children's questions. When pupils know that teachers expect questions if there are misunderstandings and misconceptions, then they are more secure and at ease in the classroom situation. The result is that they are more inclined to learn. Although this is no guarantee of learning it is certainly conducive to it. Pausing for pupil questions is the fourth craft factor.

Participation

In this step, students actually work on the lesson or activity. While they are thus engaged, it is wise for the teacher to walk among them and observe how well they are doing. Initially, however, the teacher should gather in a small group those few individuals who did not understand the presentation thus far. In this instance, the teacher should do whatever is necessary to assist them in understanding whatever they are capable of assimilating. After this activity the teacher is then free to move around the classroom and observe the balance of children who are working on the assignment. Participation is the fifth craft factor.

Evaluation

This step is actually a twofold check. The most important consideration here is to determine how well the teacher has taught and, secondarily, how well the children have learned. Since it is the primary responsibility of the teacher to teach the children in the classroom, evaluation should be focused on that point. In general, if the teacher has properly followed the suggestions given here in this explanation of the craft factors, most of the pupils will have been reached and the lesson will have been learned.

In evaluation of the type suggested here, it is best for pupils to check their own papers. The teacher could read the correct responses and let them score their own responses. This can be carried out on a small group basis or with the total class participating. In allowing pupils to correct their own work, the teacher not only places them on their honor, but also provides for immediate reinforcement. Pupil mistakes, if any, are noted immediately and appropriate corrections can be made while the information is fresh in their minds. This sixth step, evaluation, is probably the most important step because it comes immediately after students have done their work and provides them with clozure or a logical conclusion to their efforts.

Final Questioning

This last step is just as important as any of the others because it is here, immediately after the evaluation, that pupils will ask questions to find out why they made mistakes. Here is where they clarify misunderstandings and concepts which may have been marginal. The immediacy of this step also provides for greater learning. Furthermore, allowing time for final questioning tends to augment the friendly atmosphere so conducive to positive relations between teacher and pupils. Since they realize that the teacher is vitally interested in their learning and is intent on clearing up misunderstandings, students feel free to express their uncertainties. A classroom atmosphere conducive to free exchange of questions and answers is an atmosphere in which children will grow more rapidly in their learning.

In the present discussion, it is suggested that each and every pupil learning activity follow the sevenfold procedures just described. This is the proposed craft sequence of teaching to which all teachers should adhere and for which all teachers should plan. It is exact and complete without being redundant. If followed, it leads to greater learning on the part of children and this, in the final analysis, is the primary task of all teachers.

To further augment the craft sequence of teaching a planning guide is provided for your convenience. The purpose of this page is to serve as a check for you as you follow through with the craft of teaching. The guide contains those factors that are considered to be crucial in the craft of teaching because from mastery of craft comes art or creativity. This is to say that once the teacher knows how to sequentially plan an effective lesson for students, s/he is then free of the distracting need to determine teaching procedures. S/he can then concentrate on trying to develop opportunities which allow for creative and artistic teaching. Once the teacher is free from the burden of trying to figure out how to properly plan a lesson, and this becomes automatic or a second nature, so to speak, then and only then is s/he unencumbered enough to let the artistry come into teaching. It is for these reasons that the discussion of planning has been presented.

THE CRAFT FACTORS PLANNING GUIDE

The intention here is to provide the classroom reading teacher with a planning guide for each lesson. The craft factors in the planning sequence have been noted in outline form and it merely remains for the teacher to follow the steps as noted. It is recommended that teachers allow enough time for the craft factors sequence in each lesson because initially a lesson may take as much as thirty minutes. Later, when all concerned become accustomed to the process, the time involved will be less.

In using the planning guide, teachers will want to have firmly in mind the purposes of the skill building activity so that these can be explained to students. Telling them why they are going to work on an activity, that is to say, how the skill will help them as learners, is a point which is crucial to the planning sequence. This and other dialogue factors should be prepared ahead of time by the teacher as noted. Then, for the remaining factors in the planning guide all that the teacher has to do is to check off (mentally or otherwise) each step as s/he comes to it.

The following are factors for each classroom/reading teacher to consider in appraising the craft aspect of teaching all students. You may wish to ask youself each of these questions to use as a guide.

1. Introduction: Focus on purposes.
   a. Do all students understand the purposes of the lesson?
   b. Did I properly prepare them for the material? (Background)
   c. Did I explain the importance of the lesson? (Why they should do it.)
   d. Do all students understand the relationships between this lesson and other lessons they have done in the past?

2. Familiarization: Overview.
   a. Did I provide time for students to skim the material?
   b. Did I point out the relationship of this lesson with past lessons?
   c. Do all students understand the scope and content of what skills the material requires?
   d. Do I observe students as they skim the material?

3. Demonstration: Show.
   a. Have I clearly explained the procedures of the lesson?
   b. Did I effectively show students how to do the work?
   c. Were there enough examples to clearly indicate how to do it?

4. Question I: Did I pause for pupil questions?

5. Participation: Doing the lesson.
    a. Did students have enough time to do the lesson?
    b. Did I walk around the class first and help those needing it?
    c. Did I check to see how well each is doing this lesson?
    d. Were there problems that students had in doing the work?

6. Evaluation: Checking the student response.
    a. Was the lesson meaningful to the students?
    b. Did I really teach the students effectively?
    c. Did we score the responses immediately?
    d. Do all students in the group seem to understand the concepts in the lesson?

7. Question II: Did I pause for questions from the students?

7
ORGANIZATION:
The Pathway

In order to carry out the plans you have made to assist all students in reading better as noted in the previous chapter, it will be necessary for you to structure some sort of system as a framework of operation. All too frequently potentially effective reading instructional programs fall down or fail to reach their potential because they are poorly organized. And an added advantage to a good organizational scheme is that it provides all concerned with the information needed to make progress in the reading skills program. Moreover, proper organization, rather than being restrictive or confining to teachers as some may think, actually does the opposite or allows for the opposite. Good organization opens the classroom to joint cooperation, freedom of thought, a humanistic approach to learning, and helps free all members to use their own unique creative endeavors.

Unfortunately for some teachers, proper organization does not come easy and the ability to organize, just as the ability to anticipate needs and plan an effective program, demands a special perspective from the teacher. Teachers who have this ability, who organize their

This originally appeared in *Education*, January, 1967. Reprinted with permission.

classes for maximum learning impacts, may or may not be aware of what they are doing. It seems to come more or less automatically. It simply appears to be the right thing to do, so they do it.

Then there are those teachers who seem to fear organization. For some reason, they are of the opinion that if one organizes the learning environment to any great degree, then pupil learning will be stifled. And it is true that over-organization, just as with over-planning, would indeed hobble teachers and learners alike. But our discussion here is not about those extremes. We are concerned here with the optimum amount of organization, just enough to insure the smoothe functioning of the classroom/reading room learning environment.

To this end, let us examine a rationale and procedure for effectively organizing those concerned in the educational process. What is suggested below is one way to proceed.

RATIONALE

In the modern self-contained elementary school classroom of today, the teacher must work with upwards of twenty to thirty or more individual learners and try to provide them with effective instruction. All too frequently the teacher is spread thinly over the group and the educational experience is less than maximally effective. This does not need to be. The teacher can so organize students that they provide an extension of the teacher's tasks and duties. For example, in the elementary school classroom when there are tasks or specific room duties to be performed, many teachers call upon the students to help out. Moreover, most of them, when asked to participate are usually eager to comply. They enjoy this because they are faced with a practical and specific responsibility and are helping their classmates as well as the teacher. There is a certain attraction about these tasks. The pleasant feeling aroused has a salutary effect on the child and the entire group and many teachers realize this and make appropriate provisions.

Because this procedure has such positive results, it is suggested here that an enlargement of the idea would benefit all concerned. This relates to having children act as helpers in selected teaching situations. The idea is to let the students be responsible for working with their peers, to assist the teacher in learning activities that lend themselves to this procedure. There are several possibilities for such organization and one of them is noted below.

SCHOOL AS A WHOLE

As an integral part of the total school educational organization, selected older children could be used to assist others and this would be on a school-wide basis. That is to say, the entire school would be organized to provide effective assistance to others. To make it work, all students need to understand the real purposes of this service and it will have a direct impact on each classroom in the school, as well as on those in the reading room. When everyone understands what is taking place, when everyone understands what is expected, positive learning is the result and behavior problems would be minimal. Moreover, the older students who are responsible for providing much of this help could be a vital factor in assuring the smooth functioning of the school-wide program. This organization could be as follows.

School helpers could be put to use during the time before school begins in the morning. Those chosen to assist others could work in the school gymnasium, lunchroom, or special learning areas. Those needing extra help with their school work could meet there for the assistance needed. Such an organization is easily achieved.

The organized helping activity could also take place during the noon hour. Teams of helpers could eat in the lunchroom and meet with others after lunch. Or they could eat at home and return to school immediately. Then they could work with those needing help.

An after school study-help program could also be carried out and even those who ride the school bus could participate. They could meet in the study area and work until the bus came or the period ended. Those having only a few minutes to wait for the bus probably would not have time to participate. But those who usually have a long wait could benefit from studying or receiving assistance from a team helper.

This program would affect only those who wished to read, study, or increase their skills in a specific area. It would not be a requirement, but rather a voluntary activity for those who want to participate.

The total school or school-wide program is noted here because it will help establish a learning-oriented environment in the proper setting. That is to say, learning is what the school is all about and the concept of learning should be all pervasive. Furthermore, learning is not limited to what students do, each in his/her own classroom. The school as a macrostructure can provide a total learning climate if properly organized for it. Then it will be a relatively simple task to move the idea into the classroom as noted below.

CLASSROOM HELPERS

A wide range of reading achievement is shown by students in every classroom even when those students are grouped homogeneously according to some achievement measure. This variance encompasses proficiency in academic areas as well as total capacity. Some students have a high level of capability and are fortunate enough to achieve at that level. Others do not. In general, it is the students at the upper level of the learning-achievement continuum who should be called upon to aid their less able peers. Teachers should organize their classrooms so that those who have a positive attitude toward helping others can do so.

Actually, this is a twofold program. First, older children who qualify as helpers (i.e., have the desire or willingness, as well as capabilities) could visit the lower grades and help the younger children. They could work either in a quiet corner of the classroom or in some special area set aside for that purpose. The study helper would work with one or two younger students for a short period of time and then return to his/her own classroom. Second, this program is to be considered as an integral part of the self-contained classroom learning activities. This should be a flexible arrangement. Children should work together when the occasion arises rather than on a rigid schedule.

Frequently, those who achieve well usually complete their work well ahead of other children. The result is that they have extra time in which to participate in additional sound, stimulating learning activities. These rapid workers are the ones who usually should be the helpers. They have the time and frequently they also have the insight as well as a willingness or desire to assist their classmates. This resource should be utilized.

The mechanics of organizing the classroom so students can be working together could be structured in many ways. For example, when a rapid worker finished a regular assignment, he could then move to a quiet corner or special area to read a book, continue a special project, etc. This means that s/he is available to assist. A child in difficulty could go over to the area, speak with the classmate, and receive assistance. When this is satisfactorily completed, the student receiving help returns to his desk and the helper would continue with his activity. This would work well if the teachers would actually teach students how to do it.

Another organizational arrangement could be to have a rapid worker seated among several slower workers. The one in need of help could turn to the assistant, receive information, and then turn back and continue working. Conversation would be in low tones or whispers so that others would not be disturbed.

Additional arrangements to suit the teacher and children could be made as the need arose. This should be flexible and complement the physical plant of the classroom.

CORRECTING ASSIGNMENTS

As noted in the previous chapter, students should score or correct their work as soon as possible after it has been completed. The sooner this takes place, the greater the learning and the less chance there is for retroactive inhibition. And here is where the study helper can again be of considerable assistance. This suggestion is made because all too often the classroom teacher is so busy with the many educational tasks that there is seldom enough time to promptly check all completed assignments.

Today's classroom teacher usually works with three, four, or more reading groups because students vary so much in their reading achievement. Such a grouping organization is entirely correct but it means that the teacher is occupied with one group at a time and therefore it is impossible to constantly monitor all groups at once because it means being in three or four places at the same time. As a result, the student's work often cannot be checked immediately. Under these circumstances it seems very practical for the student helper to assist. H/she could take the teacher's scoring key assemble and meet quietly with a group to give the correct answers. The children would correct their own work.

Many student helpers provide valuable assistance to teachers because they have enough insight to answer questions arising from checking assignments. They may be able to explain why one answer is correct while others are not. However, this should not be expected.

A student helper is, after all, still a student. The questions which cannot be answered and the concepts which cannot be explained should be saved for the teacher who, when free later on, can answer questions and clarify concepts.

It will be noted that the teacher is not relinquishing any major teaching responsibility. Actually, s/he is providing for more real teaching time. The student helper is concerned with the mechanics of checking assignments. This frees the teacher to work with other groups. When questions arise that cannot be solved by the student helper, then the teacher takes over. In this way more teaching takes place rather than less.

It is realized that not all assignments or activities could be handled as suggested here. However, many do lend themselves to such treatment. They should receive it as noted or in some other creative and innovative organizational structure.

PROGRAM/ORGANIZATION PITFALLS

In many schools and classrooms such an organizational macrostructure to teaching has been very successful. Principals of schools, classroom teachers and reading teachers have been using a similar type of organization for many years and using it with positive effects or results. These creative and versatile educators believe that it is entirely correct to have students teach each other, score papers or worksheet responses, and assist in different ways as the situation warrants.

Unfortunately, however, there are schools, communities, and educators not yet so involved in this type of organization for learning. Those not yet so involved may be greatly confused by the sheer magnitude to the macrostructure needed to fulfill the organizational schema. Others may have severe reservations about this type of team teaching, the type that helps students become involved in their own learning. And these reservations may stem from the earnest, sincere belief that the only learning which can take place is the learning dispensed by the teacher.

So there are serious pitfalls to the organization of the school and classroom learning environment, pitfalls which cannot be readily overcome. It may take massive inservice programs to change teacher attitude and even that may not be enough, yet change must surely come about if all students are to be reached and taught to the maximum of their potential.

And there are more pitfalls. One major consideration could stem from faulty procedures which would tend to create what might be termed an elite corps in the school or in the classrooms. Teachers and children might look on the helpers as being "better" than their peers. This notion is abhorant to many in our country because it denies and is contrary to the traditional concept of equality for all.

Another pitfall could grow from the student helpers themselves. They may have the erroneous opinion that they are more important than the others they are assisting. As a result, they may seek special privileges or act in a condescending manner.

A third pitfall could be created by parents. Those whose children participate as student helpers may be inordinately proud of what is happening. This could cause other parents to be resentful.

AVOIDING THE PITFALLS

Here are some ideas to consider. The pitfalls noted above would not materialize if teachers realistically and skillfully describe the nature of this type of classroom organization. If all concerned learn about the real meaning and purposes of the team approach, the pitfalls can be avoided. Here, the key point is communication.

The teacher is the vital resource to children's insight and understanding. Here it is necessary to effectively explain certain basic concepts. One of these is service to others, a second has to do with using one's capabilities to the utmost, and a third one is learning to understand and appreciate one's peers, whatever their limitations are.

In explaining the first concept, the teacher could compare the organization of team teaching with the responsibilities of the school safety patrol or similar group. That service is usually reserved for older, more responsible children. Often they are more mature and carry out the required duties efficiently with very little personal direction.

However, not all students can do this. Some of the older ones have not yet developed such maturity and sense of their responsibilities to themselves and others. As a result, they do not participate in that special service or activity.

Yet those who do feel the responsibility and participate usually do it very well. Therefore, they are the ones who do the work and they are the ones who have grown or matured enough to do an effective job. Those who can, serve others. Those who can't don't and may stagnate.

In explaining the second concept, the teacher could use the analogy of athletics or sports. Usually it is considered sportsmanlike for a good athlete to explain to others the finer points of his/her special skill. Such sharing helps in at least two ways:

1. Those who listen learn a new or better way of doing something.

2. The person giving the explanation may gain greater insight regarding his skill.

Furthermore, under these circumstances no one is made to feel superior or inferior and the same concept applies in the organization for real team teaching as suggested here.

The third point, understanding one's peers, is another vital consideration. Children need to communicate with and understand each other. They need to realize that they are similar in some ways and different in others. They can teach each other and learn from each other. They need to know that some are slow to grow in social processes and need help in this. Others already have these concepts in adequate perspective. There is an advantage to be gained by having one type help another. This can be the foundation for acceptance, trust, mutual understanding. First of all, the slow worker will realize, among other things, that it is possible to do the work. Second, the student helper will learn, also among other things, that s/he has to be more patient and understanding of the one he is helping.

The last point is for the teacher to explain about the program. This must be done so clearly that everyone understands its nature and importance. Here it is vital for real communication to take place. Properly understanding the program will lead to effective participation by all children. Feelings of superiority and inferiority will be avoided. This will result in greater learning for all concerned.

There is no one special way for the teacher to explain the idea. However, it should be described so that children know what is to take place. Moreover, there are certain points to be noted. One of these relates to the team idea. In order for a team to function properly it must be well organized and each member must fulfill individual responsibilities. Teamwork capitalizes on the strengths of the members. Those who have certain skills and strong points should be willing to share them with others.

Once this has been explained, the teacher should note that some children complete their assignments early. This means that they have time to devote to other activities and projects. One such project could be that of helping classmates. Such assistance is not required of anyone, but it is a challenge as well as a duty. In this way, all concerned can learn and work effectively together and appreciate each other.

In this proposed organizational structure all students must be taught to understand their individual responsibilities. They owe it to themselves to make maximum use of their capabilities. Some need to seek help when they do not comprehend. Others should give help.

A final consideration relates to the amount of time children will devote to giving and receiving assistance. This should be on a flexible, rotated and occasional basis. Not all student helpers would give help all day, every day. Such a schedule would be unfair to them. Help should be given when the activity is of a more mechanical type.

A FINAL POINT

In this suggested approach to effective organization, the classroom teacher is the leader. But the teacher is not the only learning source. This is true in most learning endeavors. As such, the teacher may delegate selected activities to be executed by student helpers. This will be to the ultimate benefit of the group as a whole. Student helpers can make the most of their unique strengths and assist their classmates. Those who receive help profit therefrom. The result is that more learning accrues. And after all, this is the school's reason for being.

8
TEACHING I:
The Capstone Task

[Therapy rationale and ideas for the classroom teacher and the special reading teacher. Specific procedures to consider.]

Teachers can begin the reading therapy programs for pupils in several ways because there are many procedures open, all of which lead to growth in reading achievement. The language orientation approach is probably one of the best that we can come up with at the present. The Language Orientation Approach (LOA) consists of two parts, the first of which is the Language Experience Process (LEP), and the second is the Picture-Vocabulary-Story (P-V-S) procedure. Both have great value in helping students become better readers. Because the Language Experience Process is relatively simple in nature and easy to use in the beginning stages of reading therapy, classroom teachers and reading therapists are urged to use it as the starting point.

THE LANGUAGE EXPERIENCE PROCESS

Teacher's can begin the therapy program by providing students with many first-hand experiences. Significant experiences in and out of the classroom will have a vital, positive learning effect on students because experiences are crucial to learning to read better. Expression, both oral and written, is also crucial to learning to read better. And the Language Experience Process (LEP) capitalizes on the experiential-cognitive-expressive percepts of students, enabling them to expand their language ability.

Oral language aids students in developing their vocabulary because they use the words they have come to know through the experience. Therefore, they begin to become more knowledgeable about words and are able to think more clearly. This, in turn, helps them learn even more vocabulary so they will know even more, be more able to think at higher levels, etc. And here we have the onset of the vocabulary-knowledge-vocabulary cycle which is the first step in reading. So experiences are important.

Through first-hand experiences, pupils are brought into physical contact with a particular and selected aspect of the environment. These experiences, provide the basis for reaction, appraisal, cognition, perception and above all, discussion. As children discuss their impressions and interpretations of the experience, they share ideas orally, expressed through the use of vocabulary. Experiences then are the precursor of vocabulary development and the more experience-discussion activities the pupil has, the greater is the possibility of his learning more vocabulary. Certainly, the potential is there.

Before students enter school, they live in a world of oral vocabulary. They have learned many words and can carry on lively discussions with peers, parents, and others. But this is not reading and the transition from oral vocabulary to printed or graphic vocabulary needs to be made. That is to say, there needs to be a system of instruction which will clearly show students the relationship between speech and writing. From oral language to printed words is the transition all readers need to make regardless of their age-grade placement and the Language Experience Process will do the job nicely.

Basically, the process consists of three fundamental steps: 1) preexperience discussion or dialogue, 2) the experience in which pupils participate, and 3) postexperience discussion. And as previously noted in this text, the teacher will need to anticipate, plan, and organize or "gear up" for the activity.

Preexperience Discussion

This is what takes place before the children have the experience. In whatever they are going to do, whether it is a simple walk around the school or a trip to a location many miles away, students need to talk about it. As they speak, the teacher acts as the writer or transscriber, jotting down ideas expressed by students. Here the pupils can actually see the speech-to-print transition. Then, once the ideas are on the chalkboard, the teacher can refer to them as needed. Frequently, especially in the early reading stages, the teacher will want to repeat what is written and have the students follow along. Pointing to the words and saying them aloud helps all concerned see that one spoken word can be made into one printed word, that what has been said (and heard) can be read from its printed or graphic counterpart.

Later the teacher will want to transfere the printed material from the chalkboard to a chart and use it in subsequent reading experiences. The teacher or teacher aid could do this and when the chart is completed, students could read and reread it for the benefit of all.

The preexperience discussion and resulting language experience chart are used as tools to prepare students for the ensuing experience. The chart can be used as a guide helping the students remember why they are going on the trip and what to look for as well as how to behave, etc. So the chart has many values.

The Experience

Once the students have been adequately prepared for the trip it remains for them to go on it, to take it and enjoy a valuable learning experience. There are many learning advantages inherent in first-hand experiences. The sounds and smells are sensory experiences which aid students in making the knowledge gained more permanent. The cold of the cooling room at the milk processing plant or the heat of the furnace at the metal foundry together with the noise and clatter of machinery all add to making the experience unforgettable. There are many discussions of the language experience approach available for you to read if you wish a more detailed discussion (see, Bibliography).

Teachers are in an ideal position to make the experience not only unique and meaningful, but also to make it of lasting learning value. Here is where our modern technology comes into good use. Be sure to take the school camera along and/or have students bring their own cameras. Many of them may have instant type cameras and can take pictures throughout the trip. There will be no waiting for processing if that type is used. Also be sure to take along the portable tape recorder or video recorder because there will be many valuable sounds to hear and remember. There will be sights as well and this is where the modern portable video cameras can be used. You may even plan to take along a pocket computer or calculator to figure mileage, costs, or whatever else you can think of as valuable to compute.

From this very brief discussion of the possibilities for learning which can grow out of an experience, it is my hope that you will give serious thought to taking such trips with your students. Whatever age level you teach remember that first-hand experiences are beneficial because of the many sensory impressions they provide. Then, with modern learning aids, the experience can be enjoyed many times over by replaying tapes, reshowing pictures and rereading the experience charts.

Postexperience Activities (Charts and Stories)

This is the outgrowth of the experience after the group returns to the classroom. The procedure is similar to the preexperience chart activity because it draws upon the speech of the students as they discuss their experiences and express their ideas. The postexperience chart can be a summary of what happened and what was learned. It can be a critique of the activity noting strengths, weaknesses, and possible learning if the trip were to be repeated. So the postexperience chart can take on many different dimensions and it can serve many purposes in addition to reemphasizing the speech-to-print concept.

Another aspect of the language experience process can be carried out on an individual basis. This activity is a valuable outgrowth of the group-composed experience chart and it takes the form of a language-experience story composed by each student who wants to do it.

The language experience story is an individual effort so each one will be different, although they do have the same base or thread of thought running through them. The content of the story will be based on the thoughts, ideas, and interpretation of events as experienced and expressed by each student.

There are several ways to proceed in developing student stories and all of them are valuable enough for the teacher/therapist to consider. One activity is to simply ask each student to write his/her own story about the experience. Any words they cannot spell can be provided for by leaving blank spaces to be filled in later. This should really free the students to express themselves to their utmost. As the activity continues, the teacher can move about and assist in correct spelling as warranted. Then, those words could be put on vocabulary (3 x 5) cards for the student to learn during his/her spare time.

Another way to have students make up or author their own experience stories is to have them use the tape recorder. Here is a situation where the pupils can speak freely because they do not have to wait for the writing. As soon as thoughts come to mind they can be expressed and sometimes the rate is as much as 100 words a minute. However, in writing, even at maximum speed, the result is considerably slower, amounting to perhaps 25 words per minute if the thoughts flow without interuption. Later on, the teacher or teacher aid can transcribe the student's individual language-experience story so that it can be read by that person and also by others.

In our work with the individual language-experience story we have found one format to be of great value. First of all, it is our belief that each story should be bound in book format so that it can be placed in the classroom library. To this end we have used regular size typing paper (8½ x 11) folded in half (8½ x 5½), and we have typed the stories on the bottom third or fourth of the page. For younger students we have found that the use of the primary typewriter is best because of the large print. Two or three sentences on each lower part of the page are enough. When several pages have been typed, the manuscript is given a title which appears on the front of the book together with the name of the author.

Another phase of this bookmaking has to do with illustrations and this is why only the lower portion of each page has the text typed on it. The upper three-quarters to two thirds of the page can be used for the author's illustration of the text. The original writer must first be able to read the text on that page before s/he can draw on it. Usually this requirement presents no problem at all because the author-reader is familiar with his ideas so s/he can read it with ease. For some few students, the requirment of reading the page before illustrating it does provide an incentive to read it well.

Students really enjoy this type of reading therapy and are eager to take "their books" home to read to parents, etc. Then, after that novelty wears off, they are usually eager to "donate" their books to the classroom library so that others can read their stories. All-told this approach to the language experience process has been exceedingly valuable for all students regardless of the grade level. The process is described here so that all teachers will give it serious consideration.

This is the first step in the speech-to-print reading and language improvement process.

The special reading teacher is in an ideal position to use this approach with the students who come to the reading room for special reading lessons and activities. S/He usually works with disabled readers on a one-to-one basis where the reading improvement program is highly individualized. That type of instructional organization lends itself so easily to the effective use of this process that all special reading teachers are urged to include bookmaking in the program.

The language experience process is an initial phase of teaching students the speech-to-print concept. It is valuable for all who are near the beginning stages of reading regardless of their age level. I have used this process with students ranging from kindergarten on through middle-aged adults and it works well because it is the principal step in bridging the gap from oral vocabulary to the printed word.

There are limitations to language experience as teachers and therapists no doubt recognize from the description given above. However, such limitations do not preclude its use as noted in this text. Moreover, space does not permit a detailed description of all facets of language experience and the classroom/reading teacher who needs more information should consult the references in the Bibliography.

PICTURE-VOCABULARY-STORY (P-V-S)

The well-informed teacher/therapist is, no doubt, aware of the many suggestions and programs for reading improvement which are available for use in classrooms and clinics. There is a vast abundance of materials available and it is a big business in this country. A visit to any state reading conference will show just how much is available for reading improvement. Teachers attending national meetings such as those supported by the International Reading Association can be overwhelmed by the profusion of products to help students and others become better readers.

All ideas seem to be sincere attempts at helping pupils increase their reading proficiency and language facility. But whereas many programs have real merits they also have real deficiencies. No one, single reading or language delivery system yet suggested is perfect for all pupils under all learning conditions and this includes the language experience process noted above. However, reading and language teachers continue striving for the ideal educational programs and now I would like to explain about the process I have developed to meet this challenge.

The Picture-Vocabulary-Story delivery system or medium capitalizes on the major strengths of all reading and language approaches because it incorporates the three basic teaching methods (auditory-visual-kinesthetic), and has few of the disadvantages of previously utilized instructional programs. Teachers who are greatly interested in the challenge of helping each pupil read, listen, speak, and write to the maximum of his capabilities, should consider using P-V-S in the classroom language instructional program.

P-V-S is the product or result of many years of writing, research, reflection, and synthesis concerning the fundamental factors of reading and related language experiences. It is my synthesis of the various language processes, blending them into a viable learning activity for all who want to read better.

Basically, P-V-S is an in-depth, structured extension of the current, widely used language-experience process already described. However, there are major differences: whereas language experience is primarily a large group activity guided and directed by the teacher, P-V-S is more of an individual, partner, or small group activity needing a minimum of teacher direction and attention. In language experience teachers usually begin with the class as a whole and then move on to smaller groups or individuals as the learning occasions warrant. In P-V-S the opposite takes place. Furthermore, language-experience usually depends upon some prearranged activity such as a field trip outside the classroom; P-V-S does not because it is self-contained and is available for use at any time. Whereas language experience is limited by the nature of the activity itself and the vocabularies of the pupils, P-V-S is not. Actually, the Picture-Vocabulary-Story process tends to be almost unlimited in scope and content, depending upon the ingenuity of the teacher. Moreover, for those students who cannot work by themselves or with another pupil, paraprofessional assistance may be utilized.

In essence, the Picture-Vocabulary-Story system of instruments is a structured medium in which the pupil matches a series of cards with corresponding or related entries on one side (usually the right side) of a file folder (Illustration I). After correctly matching and aligning the cards, the folder is closed by moving the left-hand side and pressing down on it so the adhesive strip will grip the cards firmly. Then the folder is carefully flipped over and reopened (Illustration 2). If correctly manipulated, the file folder entries will appear on the right-hand leaf or page and an assembled picture, drawing, or diagram will appear, adhering to the left-hand side (Illustration 3).

Now the student can begin to use the device for his/her own learning purposes. These are usually concerned with the unique and individual thoughts of a story to go with the picture, or whatever appears assembled on the left side. Because the illustrations show vocabulary, let us consider how the student could proceed with it.

Ideally, s/he should use the vocabulary on the right and incorporate those words in the story as s/he looks at the picture on the left and thinks about its interpretation (Illustration 4). Students can tell the story orally (to the teacher, teacher aide, tape recorder, or study helper), or s/he may write a story about the picture and use the vocabulary already given or other words that come to mind from and about the picture (Illustrations 5 and 6).

The vocabulary on the right serves as a guide to lend some sort of structure to the activity. However, there is no one, single, fixed inter-

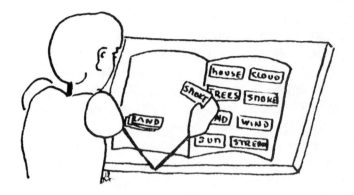

1. Student matches cards.

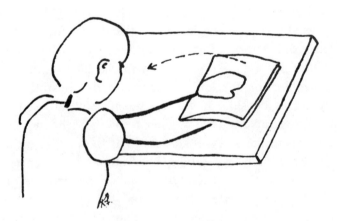

2. Folder is closed and then flipped over.

3. Folder is opened, disclosing a picture on the left and the vocabulary on the right.

4. Student studies the picture and the vocabulary.

5. Student makes up his own story using the picture and the vocabulary.

pretation which should be expected by the teacher. Instead, there should be a great diversity of responses among pupils even though the picture and the vocabulary are the same. Such is the outcome of individual interpretation of stimuli in a classroom where pupils are free to follow their own creative instincts.

Creative use of any medium depends primarily on the teacher. As such, the classroom/reading teachers should be prepared to free children to create their own stories in a manner that has meaning for them. Some will look at the picture and the vocabulary and use them as a point of departure to tell or write *their* stories as *they* interpret the medium. The result may be far different from what the teacher has expected. Such freedom of expression is to be desired.

Some students will find their interpretation leads them to draw another picture or to build something illustrative of their thinking.

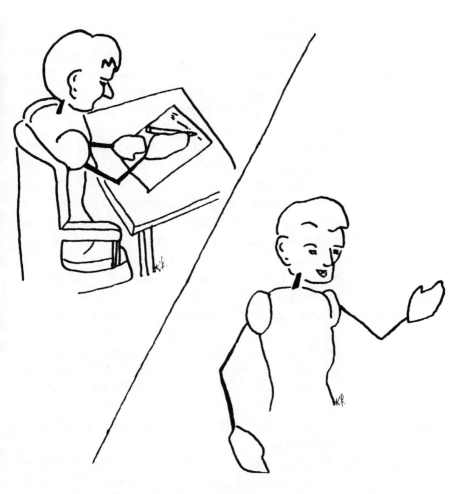

6. Pupil writes or speaks about what comes to mind from
   his experience with the device.

Again, such activity should be encouraged by the teacher. Creativity
and freedom of expression are the basic by-products of the P-V-S
medium. These ultimately lead to greater language facility, the goal
of all our instruction.

Many teachers have been greatly concerned about the possibility and probability of pupil error in matching the cards with the key items on the folder. What will happen if a student makes a mistake and places cards in the wrong space? Will this have an adverse effect as s/he tries to use the medium to improve language learning. The answer to these questions is an unqualified, "No." A pilot study, in which second graders participated, showed beyond any doubt that few assembly mistakes were made and what errors there were helped rather than hindered students.

Actually, the structure of the P-V-S medium is ideal because it provides for immediate feedback. The pupil knows right away whether or not s/he has assembled the picture correctly because if s/he has made an error, the picture will be incorrect. A part or parts of it will not be in the right place. As the student examines the picture s/he can experience visual clozure, an excellent learning experience. If an item is not in its proper place, the student can adjust it immediately, and learn from the mistake.

So, there is really nothing terribly wrong with making an error. Actually, s/he could learn more from a mistake than if none were made. Therefore, teachers are advised against being overly concerned in this matter. However, if a pupil consistently makes mistakes, it may be wise to test with visual discrimination activities to determine how serious the problem is.

The Picture-Vocabulary-Story devices are relatively simple to make and use in the classroom. This is true regardless of the grade level involved. P-V-S is applicable in the first grade as well as in the twelfth grade and beyond.

The first step is concerned with building the device. For this the teacher will be able to use readily available, more or less standard materials, easily obtained from school stores. In order to construct an instrument, the teacher will need these materials:

1. A picture that is interesting to view and that tells a story all by itself (Illustration 7). Usually these can be obtained from magazines such as *Life, Ebony, Time, Newsweek,* etc.

2. A file folder of the type readily obtained as school supplies, or in office equipment stores. The medium weight, light-colored folders are best for this purpose. Dark-colored folders should not be used because the vocabulary will not show up clearly.

3. Miscellaneous materials are also needed. These include scissors, or better still, a paper cutting board; rubber cement, or dry-mount tissue so that the picture can be smoothly mounted on a piece of medium weight, light-colored cardboard; ruler or straight-edge; marking pen, preferably black; double-stick or double-face masking tape. Envelope for holding the vocabulary and a large envelope to contain the completed instrument.

When materials have been assembled, the teacher can proceed to construct the device to be used by the pupil. First of all study the picture and decide on the nature of the story. Make notes, especially of the unusual words that come to mind as the interpretation develops (Illustration 8). Then mount the picture on the cardboard (Illustration 9). Use dry-mount tissue or some other adhesive medium so that there are no wrinkles in the picture. After that turn the mounted picture over so that the cardboard back is face up. Now look to the list of words or the vocabulary describing the picture. Divide the back of the picture into rectangles of equal size, one for each word (Illustration 10). If there are ten words for the story of the picture, divide the back into ten rectangles of equal size. If there are fourteen words which adequately describe the picture, divide the back into fourteen rectangles. Obviously this is a flexible procedure. There is no single correct number of words best suited to describe a particular picture. Actually, this depends upon the interpretation of the viewer. Such flexibility is one of the strengths of this process.

7. Select a picture that tells a story.

8. Make a list of words that come to mind.

9. Mount the picture on a piece of cardboard.

10. Divide the back into equal size rectangles.

Now that the vocabulary has been selected and the back of the picture mount has been divided into the appropriate number of rectangles, the teacher should print those words, one per rectangle, on the cardboard (Illustration 11). Care should be exercised so that the lettering is as perfect as possible. When completed, there should be a mounted picture on one side of the cardboard and the words (vocabulary), one per rectangle, printed on the reverse side.

The next step is to prepare the file folder. Open it as if it contained data or material to be perused. Hold it flat so that there is a right-hand portion and a left-hand portion facing up. Use the right-hand portion of the folder for the vocabulary list and divide that part into the same number of rectangles as on the back of the picture (Illustration 12). It may be advisable to take the vocabulary side of the picture and measure it and the rectangles containing the words so that they are of equal size. Then draw the rectangles on the right side of the folder accordingly. Once the folder has been divided into the same number of sections as the back of the picture, copy the vocabulary in the same sequence (Illustration 13). The words on the right side of the folder should be a duplicate of the words on the back of the picture. These words should be about the same size and they must be in the same sequence. At this point in the construction of the instrument, the back of the picture and the right side of the file folder look the same. The vocabulary sequence on the one match the vocabulary sequence on the other.

The next step in making this device is as follows. Take the picture with the vocabulary side face up and cut it into rectangles so that each one contains a word (Illustration 14). Using the paper cutter or scissors cut along the lines dividing the picture into rectangles. If properly cut, there will be a word on one side and a segment or part of the picture on the other side. These are the vocabulary cards which, when fitted together in the correct sequence, will form the picture on the reverse side. To check this, assemble them and simply flip the cards over. This is like a jig-saw puzzle in reverse. Finally, place the

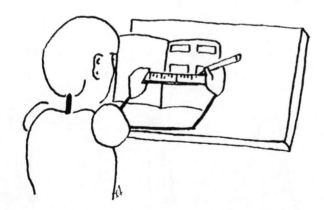

11. Print words, one per rectangle, on the cardboard.

12. Divide the right-hand side of a file folder into the same number of rectangles as the back of the picture.

13. Copy (print) the vocabulary from the back of the picture onto the folder and do so in the same sequence as on the back of the picture.

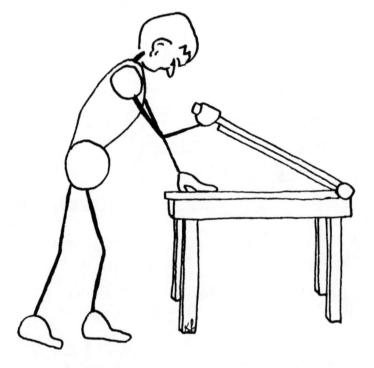

14. Cut the picture into the same number of rectangles (vocabulary cards) as appears on the back.

double-face masking tape or adhesive strips on the left-hand portion of the folder. These will help keep the finished picture in place.

The flexibility of the Picture-Vocabulary-Story medium is a major advantage to teachers and pupils alike. Each P-V-S instrument can be constructed for specific purposes or general purposes as the learning situation warrants. The construct already explained was concerned with vocabulary because this is the major function of the process originally envisioned by the author. Pupils would use the vocabulary presented for the picture and then create their own stories within that framework. Yet the medium is so flexible that is can be used in a wide variety of classroom/clinic learning situations.

In constructing Picture-Vocabulary-Story file folders for students in your classroom or special reading room you might want to consider using the *IDRT* test material described previously in Chapter 3. All of the items in the testing sequence could be adapted to the P-V-S format. Each folder could contain one skill to be learned and students needing help/therapy in a given skill could work with that specific folder.

The content for the P-V-S teaching-testing devices is already available in the Appendix of this book. All the teacher need do is restructure the items in the appropriate format.

1. **Geometric Forms.** Here the teacher can construct a "geometric forms" test-teach device appropriate to the grade level taught. Place a series of these forms on the right-hand portion of the file folder and on the back of the picture. The student can assemble the picture by correctly placing the forms and can check his accuracy by looking at the completion of the assembled picture. Three or four such geometric form P-V-S instruments should be enough to test-teach the required skills. If more are needed, the pupils themselves could construct their own for each other to use. These items are found in Appendices A-1 and A-2. How many the teacher chooses to place on the right-hand portion of the file folder depends on

the maturity level of the pupils. Perhaps a half dozen for less mature students and a dozen or so for older students would be sufficient.

2. **Letter Forms.** The same suggestions can be made for this test-teach skill. On the right-hand side of the file folder the teacher can print letters and combinations similar to those in Appendices B-1 and B-2. On the back of the picture the letters and combinations should appear in the same sequence. Again, the number of these or the amount used is left to the teacher's best judgment. (Teachers can initially make the P-V-S instruments with easily recognized letter form combinations and then go on to the less easily recognized letter forms as shown in Appendices C-1 and C-2.)

3. **Letters of the Alphabet.** Here again similar suggestions apply. Teachers can construct alphabetic P-V-S instruments of several varieties. The simplest idea would be the one-on-one where a particular letter is matched with the same one on the folder. A dozen or so letters would suffice here at any grade level. Two or three P-V-S folders could be made covering the entire alphabet.

    A more difficult alphabetic sequence P-V-S folder could be made in which a particular letter is given (perhaps the letter *e*) on the folder and the corresponding card could contain the letter before and after (in this instance *d* and *f*) with an appropriate blank space in between.

    Other variations could include the given letter on the folder and blank spaces before or after (__ fg) or (cd __). Many such sequence test-teach folders can be made by the teacher or by children in the classroom.

4. **Roots and Affixes.** This is another vital learning idea for pupils at all grade levels. Obviously, the prefixes, roots and suffixes used would be relatively simple in the lower grades and more difficult in the upper grades, but the concept is a good one to test for and teach.

The P-V-S root-affix folder could be constructed by printing a root on the folder and an affix that fits could be printed on the card. For example, *port* could be printed on the file folder and *trans* could be printed on the card. Or the opposite. Care would have to be taken that the affix would fit only one root. Suffixes and roots could be used in the same manner.

5. **Sight Vocabulary.** Picture-Vocabulary-Story instruments containing appropriate basic vocabulary could be constructed. A variation could be P-V-S synonym folders in which words are matched with others of approximately the same meaning. Then there could be the P-V-S antonym folders where word opposites are given. The flexibility of the P-V-S system is evident here because devices of endless variations can be constructed.

6. **Comprehension-Clozure.** Very valuable comprehension checks can be constructed in the P-V-S format. Teachers could print clozure type sentences on the file folder such as "The _____ _____ brought a registered letter to the house." The matching card could contain the appropriate word such as: "Mailman." Or the sentence (with the blank) could be on the card and the missing word could be on the folder. Further comprehension checks include definitions in which the word is printed on a card and the appropriate definition appears on the folder. Or vice versa. Another variation could include comprehension of mood. A short paragraph could appear on the card: "It was a dark, stormy night. John was all alone in the big house. Suddenly all the lights went out." And in the folder an appropriate word such as "fear" or "frightening" could appear. Sadness, joy, anger, etc. could be used in this same P-V-S folder.

Space does not permit a description of all the various possibilities of P-V-S instrument content. However, the examples cited above seem sufficient to help start creative teachers and pupils on the task of building a room library of Picture-Vocabulary-Story folders for all to use as testing-teaching devices. Moreover, teachers should not lose sight of the "just for fun" use of these materials. Pupils could use the devices for enjoyment as the occasion warrants.

The Picture-Vocabulary-Story system is flexible enough to include all the dimensions of augmenting any viable developmental or corrective reading instructional program. To this end these suggestions are given.

LANGUAGE FUNCTIONS AND VALUES

The Picture-Vocabulary-Story system is so structured that it incorporates all the language functions as well as specific reading skills. For example, when the teacher explains the process to a pupil, s/he has to listen carefully or s/he may miss something. When the student matches vocabulary (placing the cards over the words on the folder) s/he is using the skill of visual discrimination and is incorporating configuration clue concepts. When s/he has placed all vocabulary in the proper position, closes the folder, presses down for adhesive contact, flips it, and reopens it, s/he is manipulating the device, thereby learning greater muscular control and hand-eye coordination. As s/he views the printed words or items on the right side of the file folder and the assembled picture to the left, s/he again employs visual discrimination and the use of picture clues in concept formation. Putting it all together (synthesis) causes the child to think about or contemplate what s/he is doing and this is another valuable process. As s/he thinks about the picture and how the vocabulary can fit, s/he is using sequence and main idea concepts, all of which are crucial to reading and related language functions.

Obviously, as the pupil tells his story orally, s/he is using speaking skills which require him to formulate his ideas in some comprehensive and comprehensible form. Just as obviously, if the pupil writes his story he must also formulate his ideas in a similar manner and incorporate them and express himself in written form. The development of these skills are vital ingredients in any language learning program.

The Picture-Vocabulary-Story process can be a complete reading program by itself, but it seems better suited to the role of a vital supplementary activity. The teacher should construct several P-V-S folders or perhaps an entire series of progressively more difficult instruments for classroom use. Then explain these to the students and let them prepare their own after they understand how the medium operates. These, the pupil-prepared activities, can be shared with others in the class or with other classes and then stored in a suitable location for subsequent use as the occasion warrants. This results in a room library of pupil-prepared P-V-S instruments.

P-V-S is a flexible yet structured reading and language development activity. It has many learning advantages for teachers and pupils alike. Hopefully, teachers will utilize this new medium in their classrooms and make reading and related language functions much more appealing and worthwhile to all concerned.

SUMMARY

In this chapter on teaching as a capstone task, descriptions of two excellent learning media have been given. It was suggested that teachers and therapists begin with the language experience process (LEP) for those readers who are in the initial stages of learning speech-to-print concepts. Then, as the learners become more adept and proficient in reading and language, they can progress to the Picture-

Vocabulary-Story (P-V-S) medium which calls for higher level, more sophisticated responses from students.

To help the teacher/therapist understand the nature, scope and content of the P-V-S system, an in-depth description of the process and procedures was given. This idea is a good one because it not only includes all the positive factors of LEP, but goes beyond to make the learning experience broader and more all-inclusive.

In our next chapter, Chapter 9, teaching/therapy ideas on an individual basis are presented. Here the classroom teacher and reading therapist can learn about a viable procedure for working with students on a one-to-one basis.

9
TEACHING II:
To Individualize Therapy

[Specific suggestions or procedures to aid the classroom teacher and reading teacher who work with individual students.]

There are many ways to assist students in becoming better readers. Because all of them differ widely in their reading strengths and weaknesses, no one specific set of materials will do a satisfactory job for each one. But there are some broad guidelines we can formulate in this regard, broad procedures for therapy which will aid both the ·giver and the receiver.

As previously noted, teachers of all persuasions should anticipate student needs, plan an effective program, and organize all concerned so that the plans can be carried out. Furthermore, the best therapy is given on an individual basis so teachers should consider how to do that and it is to this end that the ideas in this chapter are aimed.

This originally appeared in *Reading Horizons,* and is reprinted with permission.

THE PLACE TO START

It has been my experience that teachers tend to begin a therapy program in one of two major dimensions. The first of these is the dimension of subject matter mastery, and the second is emphasis on a particular cluster of word attack skills (notably phonic analysis). Unfortunately, except for rare instances, neither of these provides a satisfactory solution for the reader and I should like to propose an alternative. Mastery of subject matter seldom works out to the advantage of the student because all too frequently s/he may have been "taught" the material and learned to hate it. Emphasis on a particular phase of word attack misleads the student to the point of believing that this is all there is to reading, drill, drill, drill and it is rather dull. It would seem to me that the best way for us to proceed is to think in terms of a broad plan into which we can structure the therapy and then fit the plan to the student so his/her reading needs can be met.

The Broad-Base Plan

Simply stated, this plan is concerned with helping students increase their reading speed, accuracy, vocabulary knowledge, comprehension skills, and word attack skills. The reason for this structure comes from my experience with students of all ages, experiences which have shown me that no one reads to the maximum of his/her capabilities. Even the best readers in my Reading Center, the teachers who taught there, could read faster, could learn more words, could comprehend at higher levels, and could become more habituated in dictionary usage.

So teachers in any aspect of therapy should be concerned with vocabulary improvement as a first phase because developing a large sight vocabulary for clients leads to speed and accuracy. Flash cards and the tachistoscope are valuable aids in this. The second phase of any therapy should be concerned with teaching students to understand what they read. Short stories with related comprehension checks are appropriate here. The third and final step in therapy should be concerned with teaching students the word attack skills they need in order to read independently. Teach phonic analysis, structural analysis and dictionary usage for reading independence. Each therapy session should be 30 - 45 minutes, two or three times each week. All three phases of therapy should be included in each session as noted in the broad-base plan below.

The lesson outline on the following pages may be used as a guide. It should be noted that there are two sides to the outline. Part A of the *Lesson Outline Sheet* has provisions for noting the teacher's Specific Therapy Plans. This represents what the teacher actually intends to do with the pupil for a given therapy session. It is here that we fit the broad-base plan to each student. It will be noted that there are three phases or steps to the plan and these steps represent the vital framework to be followed. It is suggested here that during each therapy session, the teacher should spend some time teaching the skills noted in each step.

1. **Developing Vocabulary Perception.** As previously noted, large sight vocabulary is crucial to reading for meaning, for rapid reading and for accuracy of word perception. To help pupils increase their sight vocabulary, the teacher should expend some three to five minutes developing this *in each session.*

   Vocabulary recognition can be developed in several ways, the two most viable means being the use of flash cards, and the tachistoscope. The teacher (or another student) could make flash cards for the student needing help. Simply print the unknown words on 3 x 5 index cards and proceed to teach the words. Once s/he knows them, more words can be added to the packet of cards.

An added dimension is provided if the teacher (or pupil helper) can riffle through the cards showing the words as the disabled reader pronounces them as fast as they are exposed. This aids the reader in the rapid recognition of vocabulary and should subsequently help him increase his general visual perception and speed of reading as well as accuracy.

The tachistoscope can be easily constructed (or it can be purchased) and used during this phase of the lesson. To construct the device simply fold a piece of cardboard in half, cut a window in one side and bind the open edge. This is the sleeve. Make a slide from another piece of cardboard and cut it so it will fit easily inside the sleeve. Carefully print or write the unknown words on the slide and insert it in the sleeve. Move the slide up so that a word appears in the window and let the disabled reader look at it for a fraction of a second. If s/he can say the word and use it in a sentence, slide the next word in place and flash it. Continue in this manner until the student knows the words or the time has expired.

If the reader does not recognize the word and cannot say it, then expose it again for a longer period. It may be necessary to teach the word by configuration and explanation as well as pronunciation. If so, recheck by returning to the word after a few moments.

2. **Developing Comprehension Skills**. This second step is the logical outgrowth of the first step and is really what reading is all about. When a reader reads, s/he must comprehend or s/he is wasting his/her time. If s/he merely pronounces words and has no real idea of what the words mean, then comprehension will be lacking. So developing reading comprehension skills is a must in any therapy session and the major portion of the lesson should be devoted to this skill.

There are many materials available and suitable for this step. The teacher (or the student) could select a story that can be read and simply have the student read it. When s/he has finished, comprehension could be checked by asking appropriate questions. Actually the process is somewhat more complicated than that and is noted as follows.

Prepare the student for the silent reading of the selection and do this by first noting or discussing some of the more difficult words to be encountered. This is preteaching the vocabulary. After making certain that s/he has some notion of what the words mean and how they are pronounced, have him/her read the story for certain purposes. S/He should have a definite goal in mind and one or two broad questions to use as guides. So, rather than simply saying, "Now read the story," the teacher could say, "Read the story to find out _____" and "Read to learn what happened to _____."

When the student has completed the story, s/he can respond to the introductory questions and give oral answers. The teacher should ask more questions in order to check on other concepts covered in the selection. It should be noted at this point that the teacher could also have the pupil read for sheer enjoyment or to summarize the selection. Not always is it necessary to have a detailed check on student comprehension. Reading for pleasure and subsequent discussion of ideas is also a worthy objective.

The reading the pupil does should be relatively short so that s/he can get through it in the brief time allotted. Ten or fifteen or, at the most twenty minutes is usually enough time to devote to developing comprehension skills during the therapy session. It is vital that this instruction take place during each session or lesson even if it means deleting part three or the last step which is the word attack skill development step.

3. **Developing Word Attack Skills.** This is the final phase of our suggested broad-base plan. It is last because I want to emphasize the need for teachers to concentrate on the first two

steps (developing vocabulary skills, and improving comprehension skills) before going on to this one. As I have noted elsewhere, too many teachers spend so much time on word attack skill development drill that students become bored and unhappy. Moreover, they learn to believe that attacking words is reading. Obviously, there is much more to the reading process and students need to realize that they must read to comprehend the author's message.

Teachers are urged to include exercises and activities in word attack skills, but to play down their importance. Students need to know how to look at a word and decode its pronunciation, but a maximum of ten minutes is recommended for such drill.

The Lesson Plan for Reading Therapy

Let us now take a closer look at the suggested broad-based plan for therapy and see how it can be adjusted to meet the specific reading needs of students. Part A of the *Lesson Outline Sheet* provides space for writing in the specific therapy plans you have made for the disabled reader. There will be different specific content for each client receiving help because different individuals have different reading needs, but the outline or the procedure will be the same.

Remember that our therapy sessions should last for about 30 - 45 minutes. In breaking the time sequence down into smaller segments, it is recommended that you devote approximately 3 - 5 minutes to developing vocabulary perception; 10 - 15 minutes or 20 minutes to developing comprehension skills; and about 10 minutes or so to developing word attack skills and dictionary usage.

To this end, the teacher should use the sheet and enter the specifics of the lesson as required. (The *Lesson Outline Sheet* may be duplicated as needed.) Write down exactly what is planned and then try to follow the plan as a guide. Also, be prepared to leave the plan if

LESSON OUTLINE SHEET

Part A: Specific Therapy Plans

Pupil's name: _____ **Date:** _____

1. Developing vocabulary perception.

2. Developing comprehension skills.

3. Developing word attack skills.

LESSON OUTLINE SHEET

Part B: Teacher-Pupil Reaction to Therapy Lesson (Evaluation)

1. Vocabulary

2. Comprehension

3. Word attack skills

the occasion warrants because there are times when the best plans will not be effective if the student is not inclined to cooperate.

Part B of the *Lesson Outline Sheet* serves a different purpose. In Part B the teacher should enter notations as to what actually took place during the therapy session. Here, then, is an opportunity for the teacher to make subjective as well as objective notations and observations about the student and how the lesson progressed.

These observations should be entered after each therapy session has concluded and the student has left. In each of the three sections note or describe what actually took place. There should be a sentence or two (or more) explaining what was done during the vocabulary phase and how the student reacted to the experience. In the comprehension part, further notations should be made as to how well this was carried out. Several sentences explaining the student's reaction and the teacher's reaction should be included here. The third section on the Word Attack Skills should receive the same treatment. How well did the student participate? How did s/he react? What progress does he seem to be making?

From these subjective observations and reactions the teacher can plan the next lesson. If the student is making satisfactory progress, then the teacher should continue. If the student is not progressing or reacting in a positive manner, the teacher can determine why and change the content accordingly.

Periodic rechecking of the initial skill deficiencies as noted in the *Diagnosis* profile should be undertaken. The time between retests should be at the discretion of the teacher. Too many tests may cause the student to become over anxious. Too few retests may result in therapy sessions which contain practice on what the student already knows and this defeats the purpose of the therapy.

The sample *Lesson Outline Sheet* shown on the following page illustrates the type of notations which are recommended. From the sample, it can be seen that each area was planned and there are goals to be met. Specific skills are to be accomplished and these build on

LESSON OUTLINE SHEET

Part A: Specific Therapy Plans

Pupil's name: _____*John X*_____ Date: ___*10/12*___

1. **Developing vocabulary perception.**

    Use the 3 x 5 flash [index] cards to review the words missed during the last session — through, because, before, could, and would.

    Continue by using the tachistoscope and teach the new words — about, first, people, only, which, where, should, back, no, an.

    Be sure to note the similarities of words (could, would, should).

    Plan to spend about four minutes at this.

2. **Developing comprehesion skills.**

    Use the *Reader's Digest Reading Skill Builders* — Level 3, Part 3, "Treasure Hunt," pp. 12-20.

    Introduce the vocabulary of the story, p. 13.

    Read the story to find out about the old pirate and what was in the trunk.

    Work on the comprehension questions at the end of the selection.

    Plan to spend 15 or 20 minutes on this.

3. **Developing work attack skills.**

    John needs more work with phonograms (word families) so plan to spend about 10 minutes with this task.

    Take the words could, would, should, and note the *ould* family.

    Then look to the new word *back*. Note the *ack* family.

    Have John make more words using *ack* (hack, jack, lack, pack, sack, tack, etc.).

    We should write these down and he should use them in sentences.

what the pupil already knows. From this point the lesson takes him/ her another step into the unknown or less well known so that s/he can grow in reading achievement.

In addition to the lesson specifics of Part A, the teacher reaction should be entered as illustrated in Part B. It will be noted that in this instance the teacher tried to help the student settle down first because he was upset about what happened to him. It is important for the teacher to be flexible and adjust instruction as the occasion warrants. It is also important to note what actually happened during the therapy session so that the teacher can determine how the student is progressing.

From this point it is a matter of continuing with the therapy sessions, adjusting instruction to fit the pupil. Although the outline for each lesson should probably remain the same, the specific content will change each time unless the student needs review or has not mastered the necessary aspects of the previous lesson.

Vocabulary may be taken from the student's reading. If s/he reads a selection and has difficulty with certain words, those words may form the base for the next therapy session.

Comprehension can be improved through the use of the appropriate exercises at the end of each selection read. Materials for this phase of the therapy session should be chosen with this in mind. Select reading materials that do have comprehension checks for the student to use.

Word attack skill development can be nurtured through the use of test results obtained from the informal tests. This is the guide, simply plan to teach the pupil so that s/he overcomes her/his deficiencies as noted. Then help him/her continue to build needed word attack skills. Again, it is recommended that the teacher use reading exercises containing such activities rather than using workbooks. The separate workbook may be distasteful to the pupil. This would be especially so if s/he has met with failure and frustration in the past.

LESSON OUTLINE SHEET

Part B: Teacher-Pupil Reaction to Therapy Lesson (Evaluation)

1. **Vocabulary.**

   John seemed upset when he came in so we talked about it. What happened was that someone kicked him on the playground. He seemed more at ease after telling me about it so we went ahead with the lesson.

   The flash card activity was very successful and he knew all the words.

   Using the tachistoscope was different. John seemed confused, so we stopped, went back to the flash cards, and then he felt better. I'll try the tachistoscope again next time.

2. **Comprehension.**

   He read the story with great interest, but had difficulty with the words measured and disappointed. I will make flash cards of those words for next time.

   The comprehension check went very well and this made him happy.

   We spent only fifteen minutes at this task and John seemed to enjoy himself.

3. **Word attack skills.**

   We reviewed could, would, and should and I noted how the *ould* part was the same. This helped in discussing the *ack* phonogram.

   John made many *ack* words and appeared to understand what he was doing, but it did go slowly.

   There was no time to write out the sentences, so we will continue that next time.

Therapy sessions should continue until the pupil has reached his potential for reading, whatever that may be. Or therapy should continue until the student reads well enough so that he can profit from regular classroom instruction.

SUMMARY

It is suggested that there are many procedures to use in therapy sessions. The teacher/therapist should use the suggestions given in this chapter because they have been successful in classrooms and in the clinical situation. A place to start was noted, a lesson outline was given, and an illustration of the procedure was included to serve as a sample. Those who use these ideas will find them to be very effective.

10
TEACHING III
From Here to There

One of the major problems we face in helping our students read better is the problem of the language itself. English has been rated the most difficult of the alphabet languages and there are several dimensions to the difficulty. Our spelling is ridiculous because we have over two thousand ways to spell the forty some sounds of English. So there is the problem of inconsistency. Yet the language is rich in words. We have more than a million of them and because of this we can state precisely and exactly what we mean.

Not only is the spelling of the language difficult, but so is its reading. The act of reading involves two fundamental skills: decoding and meaning. Actually, this is what reading is all about because the reader needs to be able to recognize a word and in the same instant grasp its meaning so that adequate comprehension can take place. To further complicate the problem, reading is not a natural act of growth, but a task imposed by society. Much stress is placed on literacy and it may make learning stressful to the student.

In order for the teacher/therapist to get from here (where the reader is at present) to there (where the reader should be in reading achievement), we should take a close look at the present state of the art and science of our mixed up language. To this end, let us examine first some of the problems associated with word attack skills.

THE PHONICS CONTROVERSY

This is a problem which seems to surface periodically and takes on the dichotomy of the nature-nurture controversy of yester-year. And a real problem that debate was. Then the proponents of heredity as the prime dictator of human growth and development had well-polished arguments for their position as did those who believed in the preeminence of environmental factors. Now in the phonics controversy the oversimplification of viewpoint is equally clear-cut. Either we teach phonics as *synthesis* or we teach phonics as *analysis,* but we probably cannot do both. However, modern phonics instructional theory and practice indicate that perceptive teachers are taking both handles and doing just that up to a point.

The Synthetic Approach

Through the process of synthesis, the reader looks at each letter of a word, says the sound of the letter, and puts the sound together with the next letter. This procedure is used with all letters or elements in the word, to the end that the reader will be able to pronounce the word when he has put all of the sounds together.

At first glance, this system might appear to work and work well for pupils attacking unknown words, words not in their sight recognition vocabulary. But all too frequently in actual practice, more confusion than enlightenment may be generated. Not only is the meaning of the word not forthcoming, but word pronunciation may be erroneous and tends to be equated with actual reading.

The problem of synthesis can be illustrated as follows: take the word *bat*. Readers were supposed to say the sound of the letter *b* first and it usually came out something like *buh*. Probably the vowel *a* gave no trouble and the reader would say *a*. So far he had *buha*. Finally, he looked at the letter *t* and probably said *tuh*. Putting all of these sounds together, he came up with *buhatuh*, which is a far cry from the sounds actually heard in the word *bat*.

The Analytic Approach

Analysis, on the other hand, called upon the reader to look at the word as a whole, to find familiar parts, and to see which phonics rules could be applied. From the known parts, the reader could determine the rest of the word providing he knew and could apply techniques such as initial consonant substitution, initial consonant blend or digraph substitution, and/or the substitution of phonograms. For example, if the reader saw the word *mat* and did not know it but did know the word *bat*, then all he had to do was substitute the sound of *m* for the *b* sound and arrive at the correct pronunciation.

Unfortuantely, this technique as with all other techniques used in our presently spelled English words, has its advantages and its disadvantages or limitations as well. Looking for known word parts or word families (phonograms) is an accepted word attack skill, but its use is restricted to those word elements that are 1) known to the reader, and 2) fit the confining pattern. Likewise, not all English words fit these nice, neat patterns because of the ridiculous and inconsistent, irregular spellings which are an ever-present roadblock to pupil reading as noted above. To illustrate the limitations of analysis techniques, take a look at the word *together*. A reader may analyze the components *to* and *get* and *her*, and not be able to continue reading because that is not the word.

Another fly in the phonic analysis ointment is the methodology based on rules. In the past, readers were taught the many generalizations and the exceptions thereto with the assumption that they would look at a word, think of the generalization(s) appropriate to it, and come up with the pronunciation. For example, the basic (and comparatively unusable) generalization regarding two adjacent vowels goes something like this: "when two vowels come together in a word, the first vowel usually takes the long sound (says its name) and the second vowel is silent." That rule is illustrated by words such as *seat, boat,* and *hail.* Recent studies have found this rule to be less than 50% effective — there are more words that do not agree (break, lead, and said) than there are that do. Moreover, a number of rules of English phonic analysis have been shown to be of considerably less utility than was once thought. So it would seem that the analysis technique using known word parts and/or phonics generalizations has also left something to be desired.

FROM HERE

This brings us to the basic question of the present dilemma, namely what is the proper place of phonics in present-day meaningful reading instructional and therapy programs? Synthesis has its limitations and so does analysis. What is the classroom and reading teacher to do?

Perhaps the best answer rests with the proper use-stress continuum. Phonics can be defined as the correct association of speech sounds with their corresponding symbols. In other words, there is a phoneme-grapheme relationship (imperfect as it is) and readers need to be taught the correct phoneme response to the appropriate grapheme. Herein lies the problem. Because of the imperfections and inconsistencies of English spellings with the corresponding lack of utility in either analysis or synthesis, how much stress should be given to modern phonics instruction in today's reading programs?

To answer this question, we must look to the actual use of phonics as the reader needs the appropriate skills to apply in attacking words. Initially, the young or inexperienced reader has a limited sight vocabulary and is faced with the problem of attacking many of the words s/he meets. So there are many printed symbol groups whose pronunciation needs to be unlocked in order for the reader to read and to read better.

The real problem, then, rests with the reader's recognition vocabulary (the store of sight words) simply because the larger the number of words s/he recognizes instantly, the easier it is to read and to comprehend. The fewer words s/he knows and/or recognizes, the more s/he will have to rely on word attack knowledge. The larger the vocabulary of understanding (recognition vocabulary) acquired by the pupil, the more effective will be the use of phonic analysis. Once the word is pronounced, the appropriate mental associations must be made with the word, then the individual can continue reading with understanding. For the reader who has a limited vocabulary of understanding, using the dictionary is the best resource. Phonics skills do not give the reader word meaning. Even if the reader can "sound out" or pronounce the unknown word through the application of phonic analysis, s/he is still unsure of the meaning and must resort to context or the dictionary. Phonic analysis does not provide word definitions. These come from the reader's previous experiences.

Mature readers follow a similar pattern. They also find phonic analysis skills of service in the pronunciation of unknown words. Such individuals usually look at words, find familiar parts, attach sounds to symbols, synthesize correctly, and come up with a pronunciation. Then, if the set of sounds is in the reader's vocabulary of understanding and s/he recognizes this from some previous experience, the meaning becomes apparent and s/he continues reading. On the other hand, even if s/he can say the word, s/he may not know its meaning. Therefore, s/he must use clues that the context may give or resort to the dictionary. Once the meaning is known, the reader can proceed until s/he comes across another unknown word. The process is then repeated.

What, then, is the real value of phonics? Simply this: the skills of phonic analysis can help when the reader looks at a word, makes the correct sound-symbol associations, and *recognizes the word* from his/her own individual store of words. If he cannot attach the sounds to meanings, no amount of phonic knowledge will help the reader understand what is read. Phonic analysis, by whatever approach used, has these limitations. Although it is considered to be the best, single-word attack skill procedure needed by readers, the value of phonic analysis is restricted and reading instructional programs should be adjusted accordingly. It is especially significant to note that reading skill instruction and therapy programs cannot be limited to phonic analysis alone. Other skill building learning procedures must be included.

TO THERE

The proper, effective, use-stress continuum regarding the teaching of phonic analysis should follow a pattern and sequence that is most beneficial to the readers needing such instruction. The foremost concept teachers should consider is that reading for meaning is the ultimate goal of all reading instruction. Mere word pronunciation, of itself, serves few real purposes. Words must be read in context and have meaning for the reader. When reading is meaning-centered, phonics can assist the reader providing the analysis skills have a firm foundation. The skills should have a solid base in order to be useful to readers. This base is made up of experiences and instruction provided by the teacher.

Initially, the skills of phonic analysis should be taught on an informal basis. Then teachers can gradually lead up to a more formal phonics program in which the skills are stressed for a time. Ultimately, however, phonics skill instruction should taper off so that the time can be devoted to other, more vital skill activities such as structural analysis, critical reading, drawing inferences and conclusions, predicting outcomes, and most vital of all, increasing sight vocabulary.

PHONICS CONCLUSIONS

It has been noted that phonic analysis is a serviceable but limited tool, or device, for helping readers pronounce words whose visual forms are unfamiliar and/or unknown. Its utility declines as readers progress through the grades. Ultimately, phonic skills have little value for readers and there is an increased need for higher level skills. Phonics most certainly does not help with the meanings of words if those concepts are unknown to the reader. In this instance, s/he must resort to use of context, the dictionary, or some other source.

The best way to help pupils become better readers is to teach them how to increase their own sight recognition vocabularies and to give them many experiences so they can learn more words. A large sight vocabulary is obtained by constant exposure to meaningful experiences and to words. This can be achieved orally (teacher-pupil dialogue; pupil listening) or visually (reading). A large sight vocabulary is retained by constant, meaningful reexposure to words (extensive and intensive reading, many experiences, and discussing experiences). A sight vocabulary is increased by continuous in-depth, in-breadth reading and more experiences at an ever higher level.

Although phonic analysis is a key of some utility in unlocking word pronunciation, getting meaning is the major purpose of reading. This phonics cannot do.

READING FOR COMPREHENSION

As noted at the beginning of this chapter, reading involves the use of decoding skills and meaning. Let us now take a look at the meaning phase and note some of the ways to assist readers as they struggle to comprehend what they read.

In the discussion of the strengths and limitations of phonic analysis, mention was made of other clues the reader must use in order to understand what the author is saying. How do some writers convey the message so that the reader does not need to use word attack skills? There are clues that authors build into their writings, clues which can be used by readers to read more or less unaided. One clue is style: If the author writes in a cogent, flowing style, pupils can anticipate which words are likely to come. This leads to the use of *context clues.* To illustrate:

> Eagerly John and Sue entered the car, fastened their seat belts, and drove rapidly all the way out to the _____ where they were to meet Dad, flying in on the noon plane from San Francisco.

Assuming the reader does not know the word in the blank space, but does know the rest s/he is able to guess at the unknown word because of them. Some words in the sentence help the reader guess at and come up with some notion as to the nature of the unknown word. Terms such as "flying in" and "noon plane" and to a lesser degree "all the way out" (airports are usually outside of town) indicate to the reader that Dad is going to come in on the twelve o'clock flight and they had better drive out to pick him up. So if the reader thinks about what is read, context is a valuable clue to understanding the message. Therefore, teachers need to teach pupils how to use it.

Another clue to word recognition is the use of pictures which accompany the printed text. Sometimes picture clues, graphs, and diagrams are valuable aids to understanding and recognizing unknown words. Of course, this depends upon the visual impression made by the picture or visual and such clues need to be taught to students in some viable manner so that they are indeed used by readers.

Sheer knowledge of a particular subject is also an important clue to word recognition. Such knowledge is represented by the stock of concepts possessed by the student and this, in turn, is represented by his own vocabulary which is related to the subject. In general, the more he knows the better he is able to read, which in turn aids him in obtaining greater knowledge which leads to a larger vocabulary, etc., *ad inf.*

So the classroom teacher and reading teacher have available many ways to help students read better. Getting from here to there is really less of a problem than might be supposed. Problems in reading the English language can be overcome by the proper and effective teaching of these clues to meaning.

But there is more. It seems fitting to end this chapter and this book with the most valuable and most controversial procedure of all. This is the cloze technique. Although a clozure test is included in the Informal Diagnostic Reading Tests as previously described, little was said about the use and the controversy surrounding word deletion in cloze selections. So let us take an in-depth look at the cloze technique.

CLOZURE AND READING FOR UNDERSTANDING

Before we describe the controversy, value, and suggested procedures for using the cloze technique, the term should be defined. No doubt there are many definitions of the cloze technique for us to consider. Wilson Taylor (1953) has defined clozure as:

> a method of intercepting a message from a "transmitter" (writer or speaker), mutilating its language patterns by deleting parts, and so administering it to "receivers" (readers and listeners) that their attempts to make the patterns whole again potentially yield a considerable number of cloze units.

So, however we think of it, the process consists of selectively and systematically deleting lexical items from printed material. This is our interpretation of clozure and it is best illustrated by the following example:

> Susan went to the _____ shop to buy several almond rolls.

In reading this sentence, one can easily supply the missing word by using context as a guide. In order to understand where Susan went, the reader needs to decode and comprehend the entire sentence. When this is done, the sense of the sentence is clear and the missing word readily brought forth. In the present illustration the word bakery is probably the first word to come to mind. If not bakery, then the word "bake" or "pastry" may be considered.

But let's take another look at the same sentence with a different word deleted:

> Susan went to the pastry shop to buy several _____.

From this we can understand that a variety of words fit because Susan could buy any number of goodies at the pastry shop. In addition to, or in place of, the almond rolls, she could buy doughnuts, lemon cookies, brownies, etc. So what we are suggesting here is that the cloze technique enjoys the advantage of being rigid or flexible depending on the position of the word deleted from the sentence. Moreover, these deletions are under the control of the reading teacher/ therapist and can be adjusted precisely to suite the cognitive/vocabulary deficiencies of the student needing help.

A Cloze Controversy

The lexical deletions may appear simple and straightforward because there seems to be few problems associated with word removal. But such is not the case. Well-respected authorities in the field of reading believe that major problems do arise when one considers the frequency of deletions for cloze technique purposes. There are those who are of the opinion that every fifth word should be removed from the passage and if we consider this and our sentence about Susan, we have:

Susan went to the _____ shop to buy several _____ rolls.

Could she go to the *electrical* shop for *wire* rolls? She could also go to the *machine* shop and buy *wire* rolls, or to the *fabric* shop for *double-knit* rolls, etc., *ad inf.* And if she did, what does this do to the original context? So, I would like to recommend that you delete every tenth word (or approximately every tenth word) in your therapy passages because the purpose is to aid the students who need successful reading experiences. You should want your readers to supply the original lexical deletions and, once the prose passage is understood, then they can go on to supply other words in an attempt to expand their vocabulary.

Another procedure to note here — a procedure suggested by Professor John Merritt — is the use of initial consonants (or blends/

digraphs) as an aid to reader comprehension. Some readers need this help and the following will serve to illustrate the point.

> Susan went to the b＿＿＿＿＿＿ shop to buy several almond rolls.

The initial consonant offers the reader a valuable clue to the missing word. It may be obvious and it may be too much assistance, but some readers need this help, so we should use it as the occasions warrant.

Reading and Cognition

Reading authorities would probably agree that the most important goal for a reader is to grasp the meaning of the material being read. So, the purpose of reading is to understand the author's message. To do this, several skills are needed for the various levels of thinking required of the reader. According to Bloom and Krathwohl (1956), levels of cognition from the highest to the lowest, include the following:

- Evaluation — the level at which judgments are made.

- Synthesis — pulling together all elements of the material.

- Analysis — discerning the components and their relationship.

- Application — being able to take an idea and relate it to concrete situations.

- Comprehension — understanding an idea but not grasping all implications.

- Knowledge — *lowest* level where facts are garnered.

And for some students, even the lowest level is difficult to achieve. But we should try to achieve it for them and then help them go beyond that point so that reading becomes an enjoyable as well as successful experience for them.

In order for us to assist our poor readers in understanding printed material, we focus our therapy sessions on the development of three skill clusters. Our efforts are directed toward the improvement of 1) vocabulary skills, 2) comprehension skills, and 3) word attack skills. We have found that these are the major deficiencies of our clients at all levels.

METHODOLOGY AND CLOZURE

A typical therapy lesson follows the three-step format noted above: vocabulary development, comprehension improvement, and word attack activities including dictionary work. An example of this is illustrated as follows.

Initially the therapist will examine a prose selection prior to its reading by the client. In the perusal, the therapist selects pertinent vocabulary to pre-teach so the reader will be acquainted with potentially difficult terms. Let us look at the story of Susan and see how this could work out.

It was a beautiful spring day. Susan went to the bakery shop to buy several almond rolls. She was thinking ahead to the afternoon when David, her fiance, was going to have tea with her. The delicious odors present in the shop caused her some confusion because they all smelled so good. What else should she buy? What other pastry might David enjoy? Was there some item on special sale for the day, something new that would be worth trying? It was very difficult for Susan to decide on what to buy.

In our story, the therapist could select many words, depending upon the vocabulary knowledge of the client. For illustrative purposes let us use these: *bakery, almond, fiance, confusion, special, difficult,* and teach them to the client before he reads the story. Such teaching may be carried out by using vocabulary cards (3 x 5 index cards) which are flashed (or used untimed) or by using a small cardboard (handmade) tachistoscope. Usually, in our therapy sessions, the vocabulary is pretaught, untimed and then flashed using the cards or hand tachistoscope. This takes upwards of five minutes.

For step two of the therapy session, the step in comprehension improvement, we usually ask the client to read the selection silently after s/he has had an opportunity to look over the questions to be used as a reading guide. We have found this to be a valuable change from the "traditional" therapy program, a program in which the client reads aloud a selection and then answers questions. We present the questions first, discuss them, and then have the client read silently to find the answers.

In our illustration, questions such as these could be used:

1. Where did Susan go?

2. Why did she go there?

3. What caused her confusion?

4. Why did she look for a special sale item?

5. What does the word "delicious" mean? "confusion"?

We try for a few questions requiring factual information, a few requiring higher level cognitive processes, and some questions as to the meaning of vocabulary. Obviously, other questions could be asked, but the examples given above serve to illustrate our series. Then, over a period of time as the various lessons continue, other types of questions are asked so that all together, the reader is called upon to develop all levels of cognitive response.

The next step is reading the selection as a cloze passage. That is to say, the same material is transcribed with every tenth (or so) word deleted. The client is to read the story and supply the original word.

Then he reads it again and supplies other words that could fit the text.

Transcribed into the cloze technique our story of Susan could very well emerge as:

It was a beautiful spring day. Susan went to the _____ shop to buy several almond rolls. She was thinking _____ to the afternoon when David, her fiance, was going to have _____ with her. The delicious odors present in the shop caused her some _____ because they all smelled so good. What else should she _____? What other pastry might David enjoy? Was there some _____ on special sale for the day, something new that would be worth _____? It was very difficult for Susan to _____ on what to buy.

The client is required to respond with the original vocabulary: *bakery, ahead, tea, confusion, buy, item, trying, decide,* and when this is accomplished successfully, he is required to suggest other words that could fit. Alternative vocabulary elicited from the client could include: *pastry, bake; forward, then; tea, a snack; dismay, problem; purchase, select, include; pastry, cake, baked goods; buying, selecting; settle, think of;* and the result would be an enlarged vocabulary for the client. This part of the lesson takes from 20 to 30 minutes of the therapy sessions.

The third step in the reading lesson takes from 5 to 10 minutes and is concerned with word attack skills and/or dictionary usage. If the client needs phonic analysis drill, structural analysis activities, dictionary use knowledge, or other skills, these are then presented to him/her for the remaining time in the therapy session. Because such activities can take so many different forms it is difficult to discuss all possible illustrations in this limited space. Clients could work on syllabication skills, initial consonant (blend/digraph) substitution, phonogram substitution; root and affix activities as well as dictionary skills, etc., *ad inf.* The specific nature of this part of the therapy session is dictated by the specific needs of the client.

SUMMARY

In our therapy sessions (45 - 60 minutes) we follow a three step approach for our adult (and nearly adult) readers. Step one is concerned with the preteaching of the vocabulary of the selection the client will read. For this we use flash cards and the tachistoscope. This phase takes about five minutes. Step two is concerned with reading for comprehension. We have the client read the check-up questions first so that he has some specific (and broad) purposes for reading. Then he reads the passage silently and, when completed, answers the questions. In the second part of step two we have the client read the passage again, but here the text has been transcribed into cloze format. The client must supply the original word initially, and afterwards think of other words that could fit the context. This phase takes from 20 - 30 minutes. In step three we require clients to learn word attack and dictionary skills specifically designed to overcome their deficiencies. This phase takes from 5 - 15 minutes, but no more and it must be the third step.

Rationale

We use the therapy sequence so that we can stress vocabulary and comprehension development. All too frequently therapy sessions are nothing more than drill on word attack skills. As a result, the reader grossly misinterprets the reading process and believes it to be skill drill rather than a meaning getting process. We do not want our teachers to fall into this trap.

Bibliography

Austin, Mary C., et al. *The Torch Lighters: Tomorrow's Teachers of Reading.* Cambridge, Massachusetts: Harvard University Press, 1961.

Balyeat, Ralph & Norman, Douglas. "LEA-Cloze-Comprehension Test." *The Reading Teacher,* 28:555-560, March, 1975.

Bloom, Benjamin & Krathwohl, David R. "Taxonomy of Educational Objectives." *Handbook I: Cognitive Domain.* New York: David McKay Co., Inc., 1956.

Boyd (sic), Bruce A. "Teaching as a Science." *Education,* 90:63-64, 90, September-October, 1969.

Buros, Oscar K. *The Sixth Mental Measurement Yearbook.* Highland Park, New Jersey: Gryphon Press, 1965.

Blanton, William E., et al. (Eds.) *Measuring Reading Performance.* Newark, Delaware: International Reading Association, 1974.

Clymer, Theodore. "The Utility of Phonics Generalizations in the Primary Grades." *The Reading Teacher,* 16, January, 1963.

DeBoer, Dorothy L. (Ed.) *Reading Diagnosis and Evaluation.* Newark, Delaware: International Reading Association, 1970.

Durr, William K. (Ed.) *Reading Difficulties: Diagnosis, Correction, and Remediation.* Newark, Delaware: International Reading Association, 1970.

Durr, William K. (Ed.) *Reading Instruction Dimensions and Issues.* Boston: Houghton-Mifflin Company, 1967.

Ekwall, Eldon E. *Diagnosis and Remediation of the Disabled Reader.* Boston: Allyn and Bacon, Inc., 1976.

Harris, Albert J. & Sipay, Edward R. *How to Increase Reading Ability* (6th Ed.). New York: David McKay Company, Inc., 1975.

Heilman, Arthur W. *Principles and Practices of Teaching Reading.* Columbus, Ohio: Charles E. Merrill Books, Inc., 1977.

Jongsma, Eugene. *The Cloze Procedure as a Teaching Technique.* Newark, Delaware: International Reading Association, 1971.

Lindvall, C. Mauritz & Nitko, Anthony J. *Measuring Pupil Achievement and Aptitude* (2nd Ed.). New York: Harcourt, Brace, Jovanovich, Inc., 1975.

Lloyd, Bruce A. "Real Team Teaching." *Education.* 87:296-300, January, 1967.

Lloyd, Bruce A. "The Phonics Quagmire." *Reading Horizons,* 10:19-23, Fall, 1969.

Lloyd, Bruce A. "A Second Grade Experiment with a New Reading-Language Process." *Reading Horizons.* 15:142-146, Spring, 1975.

Lloyd, Bruce A. "A Reading Improvement Program for Mature Adults." *Forum for Reading.* 6:26-35, November, 1976.

Mager, Robert F. *Preparing Instructional Objectives.* Palo Alto, California: Fearon Press, 1962.

Mager, Robert F. & Beach, Kenneth M. Jr. *Developing Vocational Instruction.* Palo Alto, California: Fearon Publishers, 1967.

Mager, Robert F. *Developing Attitude Toward Learning.* Palo Alto, California: Feron Publishers, 1968.

Marzano, Robert J. et al. "The Graded Word List is Not a Shortcut to an IRI." *The Reading Teacher,* 31:647-651, March, 1978.

McGinitie, Walter H. (Ed.) *Assessment Problems in Reading.* Newark, Delaware: International Reading Association, 1973.

McKee, Paul. *Reading: A Program of Instruction for the Elementary School.* Boston: Houghton-Mifflin Company, 1966.

McKenna, Michael. "Synonymic versus Verbatim Scoring of the Cloze Procedure." *Journal of Reading,* 20:141-43, November, 1976.

Mills, Robert E. *Learning Method Test.* Ft. Lauderdale, Florida: The Mills School, 1970.

Morrison, Coleman & Austin, Mary C. *The Torch Lighters Revisited.* Newark, Delaware: International Reading Association, 1977.

Salvia, John & Ysseldyke, James E. *Assessment in Special and Remedial Education.* Boston: Houghton-Mifflin Company, 1978.

Smith, Chauncey W. & Chapman, Reuben. *Accountability: A Management Tool for Teachers.* Lansing, Michigan: State of Michigan Department of Public Instruction.

Spache, George D. *Diagnosing and Correcting Reading Disabilities.* Boston: Allyn and Bacon, Inc., 1976.

Spache, George D. & Spache, Evelyn. *Reading in the Elementary School* (4th Ed.) Boston: Allyn and Bacon, 1977.

Standal, Timothy C. "Readability Formulas: What's Out, What's In?" *The Reading Teacher,* 31:642, March, 1978.

Taylor, David R., Govatos, Louis A. & Lloyd, Bruce A. *Evaluation of Undergraduate Preparation in the Teaching of Reading* (Final Report). Kalamazoo, Michigan: College of Education, Western Michigan University, October, 1970.

Taylor, Wilson L. "Cloze Procedure: A New Tool for Measuring Readability." *Journalism Quarterly,* 30:415-33, Fall, 1953.

Zintz, Miles V. *Corrective Reading* (3rd Ed.). Dubuque, Iowa: Wm. C. Brown Company, Publishers, 1977.

APPENDICES

APPENDIX A-1
Visual Discrimination I.

Make 4" x 11" flash cards containing simple geometric forms such as circles, squares, diamonds, etc. and have students draw the one that does not belong.

APPENDIX A-2
Visual Discrimination I.

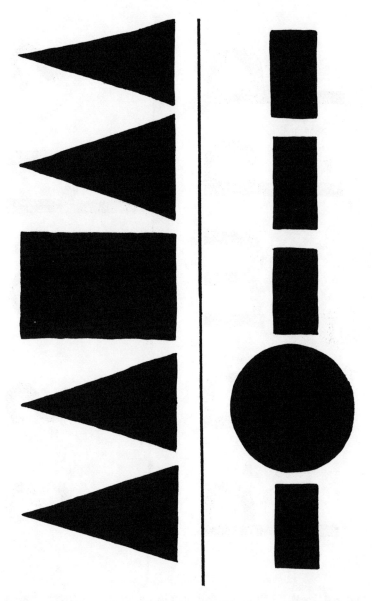

Make 4" x 11" flash cards containing simple geometric forms such as circles, squares, diamonds, etc. and have students draw the one that does not belong.

APPENDIX B-1
Visual Discrimination II.

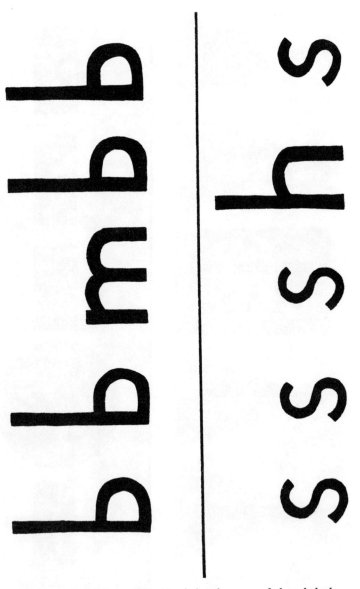

Make 4" x 11" flash cards containing letters of the alphabet such as "b b m b b" or "s s s h s" and have students draw the one that does not belong.

APPENDIX B-2
Visual Discrimination II.

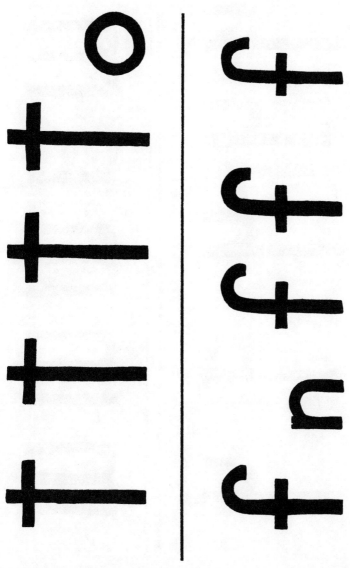

Make 4" x 11" flash cards containing letters of the alphabet such as "b b m b b" or "s s s h s" and have students draw the one that does not belong.

APPENDIX C-1
Visual Discrimination III.

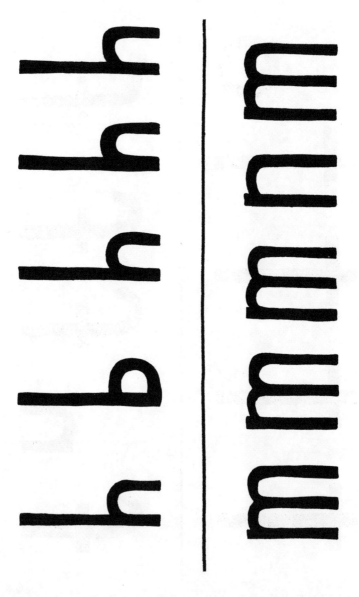

Make 4" x 11" flash cards containing alphabet letters that are more difficult to distinguish such as "h b h h h" or "m m n m m" or "o o o o a" and have students draw the one that does not belong.

APPENDIX C-2
Visual Discrimination III.

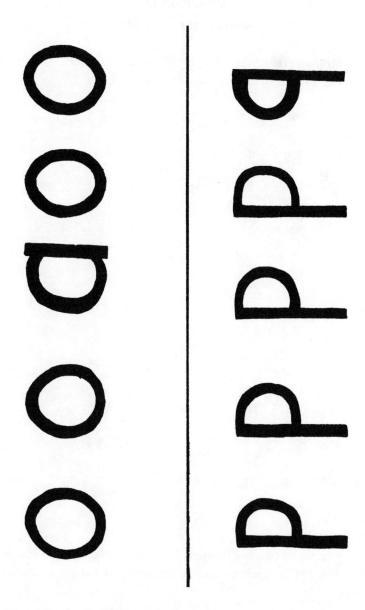

Make 4" x 11" flash cards containing alphabet letters that are more difficult to distinguish such as "h b h h h" or "m m n m m" or "o o o o a" and have students draw the one that does not belong.

APPENDIX D
Letters of the Alphabet I.

Directions: Have the student name these letters. Do not have him say the sounds of the letters, just name them.

t   g   x   n   a   h   p   v   k   o

r   z   j   q   f   s   d   y   m   c

e   w   l   u   i   b

Now name each of these letters:

U   L   I   B   E   W   C   M

D   Y   S   F   Q   J   Z   R   O

K   V   P   H   A   N   X   G   T

On a separate sheet of paper, have the student write the letters of the alphabet in their proper order. Have him do it as quickly as he can.

For scoring purposes, record only the score in naming the lower case letters. Enter score as subtest 4 on the Profile-At-A-Glance.

APPENDIX E
Letters of the Alphabet II.

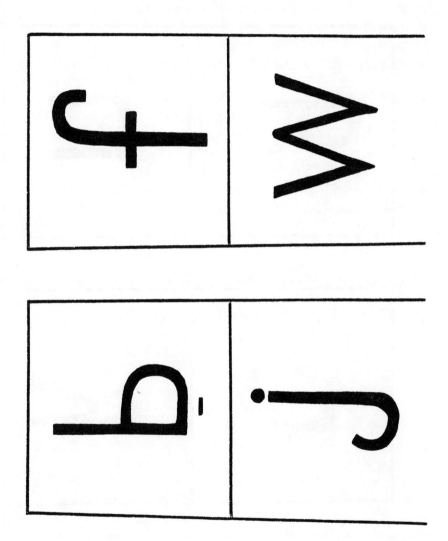

This is to check to find out if students know the letters of the alphabet in sequence from a given point. Make 4" x 4" flash cards of letters such as "b d f l p t w" and have students write the next two letters which follow the letter they have seen. (Show the letter "f" and students should write "f-g-h", etc.)

APPENDIX F
Letters of the Alphabet III.

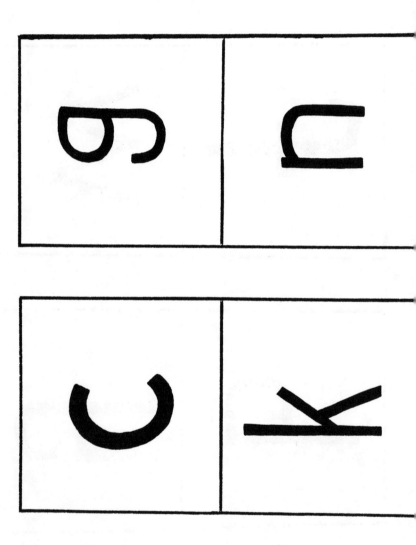

This is a check to learn whether students know the letters of the alphabet before and after a specific letter reference point. Make 4" x 4" flash cards of letters such as "c g k n r v" and have students write the letters that come before and after the letter they have seen. (Show the letter "k" and students should write "j-k-l", etc.)

APPENDIX G-1
Auditory-Visual Discrimination IV.

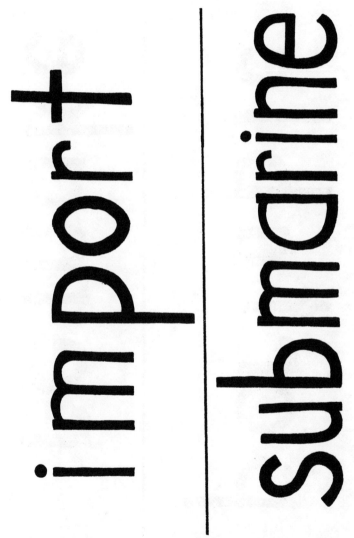

Make 4" x 11" flash cards containing words with roots and affixes. Have students copy the words, underline the root word twice, and the prefix or suffix once.Use words such as import, submarine, portable, remake, placement, formless, transportable, replaceable, nonsense, and disassembling.

APPENDIX G-2
Auditory Visual Discrimination IV.

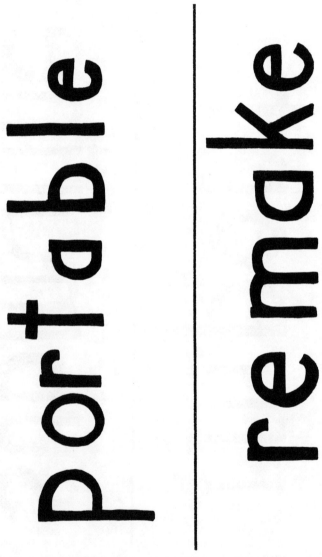

Make 4" x 11" flash cards containing words with roots and affixes. Have students copy the words, underline the root word twice, and the prefix or suffix once. Use words such as import, submarine, portable, remake, placement, formless, transportable, replaceable, nonsense, and disassembling.

APPENDIX H-1
Basic Sight Vocabulary Test: Part I

Name _____ Date _____

1. the	of	and	each
2. was	just	for	it
3. because	in	that	is
4. with	as	his	on
5. be	at	by	should
6. this	had	not	are
7. but	from	or	have
8. an	they	which	one
9. you	were	her	all
10. she	their	would	we
11. him	been	has	there
12. when	who	will	more
13. those	if	out	so
14. said	what	up	its
15. about	into	than	them
16. can	only	other	new
17. some	could	time	these
18. two	may	then	do
19. first	any	my	now
20. such	like	our	over
21. man	people	even	most
22. made	after	also	did
23. many	before	must	through
24. back	years	where	much
25. your	draw	well	down

If you give the test to an individual, you will need a copy and so will the pupil. Simply have him read off each word in a row and as he does so, record the correct responses by making a check mark and the errors by writing in the word as said by the pupil.

APPENDIX H-2

Basic Sight Vocabulary Test: Part II

Name ———————————————————— Date ——————————

1. look	little	state	good
2. very	make	would	still
3. own	asked	men	work
4. long	late	there	between
5. both	life	being	under
6. never	day	same	another
7. know	while	last	might
8. eyes	great	old	year
9. off	come	since	against
10. going	came	right	used
11. take	three	states	himself
12. few	house	use	during
13. without	again	place	American
14. around	however	home	small
15. found	Mrs.	thought	went
16. find	part	once	general
17. high	upon	school	every
18. don't	does	got	united
19. left	number	course	night
20. until	always	away	something
21. fact	though	water	less
22. public	put	thing	almost
23. hand	enough	called	took
24. head	yet	system	government
25. better	set	told	nothing

If you give the test to a group, each student will need a copy and you may proceed as follows: read one word in each row and have the students underline the word you said. When Part I has been completed, students are ready for Part II.

APPENDIX I

Reader – Cloze Technique: Level I

Once upon a time there was a boy _____1_____ Jim. He had dark brown hair and _____2_____ eyes. He was a nice _____3_____ most of the time.

One day Jim and _____4_____ family moved to a new house in a new _____5_____. Jim thought that the new people might not like _____6_____. He did not go away from his new _____7_____.

"Oh, dear," said Jim, "I wish I had not _____8_____ to this new city."

"I am afraid that the people will not _____9_____ me."

His mother asked him, "Why don't you play with that _____10_____ boy next door?"

Jim said, "Maybe he will not like _____11_____."

"But I wish I could make a snowman with _____12_____."

"Of course he will like you," said Mother, "Why shouldn't _____13_____?"

So Jim went to play with the _____14_____ next door.
They both had a very good _____15_____.

Begin with the first selection and have the pupil read the passage silently. As he reads he should be able to comprehend the passage and fill in the missing word.

After the student has successfully completed the first selection, have him attempt the next one. Continue this until he can no longer understand what he is reading. Seventy-five percent accuracy is acceptable for each Clozure selection.

APPENDIX J

Reader — Cloze Technique: Level II

Mike, Dot and Joe live in a city. It is not a big or large ___1___. It is just large enough to have a ___2___ with many fine animals in it.

Mother said, "Mike, Dot and Joe, you cannot wash the ___3___ now. Father wants to drive us somewhere."

Father said, "It is a nice sunny day. Who would like to ___4___ to the zoo?"

"I would," said Mike.

"I would," said Dot.

"I ___5___," said Joe, "and we can wash the car ___6___."

Father said, "I have an idea. Let us get a fast car ___7___ on the way to the zoo."

"That is a good ___8___," said Mother.

"Yes," said the children, "that is a ___9___ good idea."

Mother said, "I cannot go with ___10___. We are having some friends over ___11___ dinner."

"You go to the zoo and I will stay ___12___ and cook."

So off to the zoo went Father and the ___13___ in their car.

They had a good ___14___ at the zoo.

They did not want to go ___15___.

The student may say the word orally or he may write the missing word in the blank space. You may wish to have him write the answer on a separate sheet of paper and this is also permissable.

APPENDIX K

Reader – Cloze Technique: Level III

The boy's clubhouse was built in the center of ___1___ vacant lot. That was just the right ___2___ for it. Three boys built the clubhouse and their own ___3___ were the same distance away. Jim's house was behind the ___4___. John's house was on the other side. Joe's ___5___ was sort of inbetween.

Last summer the boys ___6___ the clubhouse with old pieces of lumber some workmen gave ___7___. The clubhouse was not much to look at. It sagged. It ___8___ when the wind blew. The door was so small the boys had to crawl to get ___9___. It was small. It was so ___10___ that there was barely enough room for all three of them.

In fact, it was so small that Jim's collie ___11___ had to stay outside. That always bothered Shep because he ___12___ he was a club member.

It was not long before the boys ___13___ to build a new clubhouse. This time they would make it much ___14___. Then all of them, including Shep would have more ___15___.

Many students may wish to read the entire selection first in order to have an overview of it. Then they can go back to the beginning and insert the word that fits the context. Other students may want to read several sentences before responding. This is the correct way to proceed because it indicates that students are using context clues and this is what they should do.

APPENDIX L

Reader — Cloze Technique: Level IV

One nice morning in June two boys went for a hike on ___1___
prairie. Spring was late in coming that ___2___. Pure white snow-
drifts still clung to the steep ___3___ of the river. More snow could
be seen in the shelter of large maple ___4___. The river was very
cold and icy with the ___5___ snow that ran down into it. There
was cold air rising from the ___6___ as it made its way through the
prairie. But there was a gentle ___7___ blowing over the land. It
brought the ___8___ of spring and the boys were happy. They were
looking ___9___ to summer and to the time when they made long
hikes on the ___10___.

Now the spring wind blew gently and it made them ___11___
faster. They were in a hurry to reach some high ground where there
___12___ a fence post. They wanted to climb the fence ___13___
because from that position they could look out over the prairie and
see for ___14___ miles. This is because the land was so ___15___.

APPENDIX M

Reader — Cloze Technique: Level V

John left Chicago in the month of April. He had saved money from ___1___ magazine subscriptions. He had saved fifty ___2___ and wanted to see some of the country. In his back-pack he had his ___3___ and some tools. He had a knife and an ___4___ for chopping wood. He had a frying ___5___ to cook his meals. In place of matches he had a flint and steel to start a ___6___. The man who sold him that at the ___7___ also showed him how to use it. The man gave John a little pouch in which to ___8___ the flint and steel. To catch the sparks he gave ___8___ some tinder. Then he told John that if he should run out of ___10___ he could shred cloth and use that.

So John started on his journey through the ___11___. He walked for many miles and saw many interesting things. The most ___12___ thing he saw were the state parks. In some of them he could ___13___ overnight. He greatly enjoyed being out of doors and sleeping under the ___14___. When it came time for him to return home he was ___15___ very happy.

APPENDIX N

Reader – Cloze Technique: Level VI

Many people who have seen pictures of the huge steel ships and atomic submarines of the United States ____1____ may find this difficult to believe. Years ago our mighty navy consisted only of a few wooden ____2____. This was during the time of the Revolutionary ____3____ way back in the eighteenth century. One of the first great American naval ____4____ was John Paul Jones. He was a great man whose courage and daring stand ____5____ in history. From his action and patriotism came some of the ____6____ traditions of the Navy. John Paul Jones was a real hero of yesteryear. ____7____ was born in Scotland in 1747 and was the ____8____ of a poor gardner. When he was a small ____9____ he always enjoyed a visit to the seaport near his ____10____.

He especially liked to look at the many different ____11____ that came to the port. He watched them as they rode at ____12____ in the harbor. Many sailors came to the port and John Paul Jones ____13____ friends with them. The sailors seemed to like this alert, friendly boy who always asked ____14____ about the sea and the ships. Usually the sailors were eager to ____15____ his questions and John learned much from them.

APPENDIX O

Reader — Cloze Technique: Suggested Responses

Level I

1. named, called
2. blue, brown
3. boy, fellow
4. his
5. city, town
6. him
7. home, house
8. come, moved
9. like
10. nice, new
11. me, us
12. him
13. he
14. boy
15. time

Level II

1. city
2. zoo
3. car
4. go
5. would
6. later
7. wash
8. idea
9. very
10. you
11. for
12. home, here
13. children
14. time
15. home

Level III

1. a
2. place
3. homes, houses
4. lot
5. house, home
6. made, built
7. them
8. shook, leaned
9. in, through
10. small
11. dog (name)
12. thought
13. had, wanted
14. larger, bigger
15. room, space

Level IV

1. the
2. year
3. banks, sides
4. tree
5. melted
6. river, stream
7. breeze, wind

Level V

1. selling
2. dollars
3. clothing
4. ax
5. pan
6. fire
7. store

Level VI

1. navy
2. ships
3. War
4. heroes, leaders
5. out, forth
6. present
7. He

Level IV (cont'd)	**Level V** (cont'd)	**Level VI** (cont'd)
8. smell, hint	8. keep, store	8. son
9. forward, ahead	9. John, him	9. boy, lad
10. prairie	10. tinder	10. home
11. walk	11. country	11. ships
12. was	12. interesting	12. anchor
13. post	13. camp	13. made, became
14. many	14. stars	14. questions
15. flat	15. not	15. answer

APPENDIX P

Selected List of Teacher Resources

BARNELL-LOFT PUBLISHERS
958 Church Street
Baldwin, New York 11510

BENEFIC PRESS
10300 W. Roosevelt Road
Westchester, Illinois 60153

BOWMAR PUBLISHING CORP.
622 Rodier Drive
Glendale, California 91201

CALIFORNIA TEST BUREAU DIV.
 McGraw-Hill Book Company
Del Monte Research Park
Monterey, California 93940

CONTINENTAL PRESS, INC.
Elizabethtown, Pennsylvania 17022

DEXTER AND WESTBROOK, LTD.
111 South Center Avenue
Rockville Center, New York 11571

EDUCATIONAL DEV. LAB., INC.
Huntington, New York

ERIC/CRIER CLEARINGHOUSE
1111 Kenyon Road
Urbana, Illinois 61801

JAMESTOWN PUBLISHERS
P. O. Box 658
Portland, Maine 04101

INTERNATIONAL READING ASSN.
800 Barksdale Road
Newark, Delaware 19711

McCORMICK-MATHERS PUBLISHING CO.
450 W. 33rd Street
New York, New York 10001

CHARLES E. MERRILL PUBLISHING CO.
1300 Alum Creek Drive
Columbus, Ohio 43216

NATIONAL EDUCATION ASSOCIATION
1201 16th Street, N. W.
Washington, D. C. 20036

F. E. PEACOCK PUBLISHERS, INC.
401 West Irving Park Road
Itasca, Illinois 60143

PSYCHOTECHNICS INC.
1900 Pickwick Avenue
Glenview, Illinois 60025

READER'S DIGEST SERVICES, INC.
Educational Division
Pleasantville, New York 10570

SCHOLASTIC PUBLICATIONS
904 Sylvan Avenue
Englewood Cliffs, New Jersey 07632

SCIENCE RESEARCH ASSOCIATES, INC.
259 East Erie Street
Chicago, Illinois 60611

WEBSTER DIVISION
McGraw-Hill Book Company
Manchester Road
Manchester, Missouri 63011

WISCONSIN DESIGN FOR READING SKILL
Interpretive Scoring Systems
4401 W. 76th Street
Minneapolis, Minnesota 55435

APPENDIX Q

References: Free or Inexpensive Materials*

Teachers frequently require additional instructional materials to use with their students. However, with the increasing cost of reading aids, many are severely restricted in what they can afford to purchase.

Plan to use the free or economical materials which are described in the following reference books:

Charles DuVall and Wayne Krepel, **EDUCATOR'S INDEX OF FREE MATERIALS** (86th Edition). Randolph, Wisconsin: Educator's Progress Services, Inc., 1978.

Norman R. Moore (Ed.), **FREE AND INEXPENSIVE LEARNING MATERIALS** (18th Edition). Nashville, Tennessee: Peabody College for Teachers, 1976.

Robert Monahan, **FREE AND INEXPENSIVE MATERIALS FOR PRESCHOOL AND EARLY CHILDHOOD.** Belmont, California: Fearon Publishers, 1973.

Bonnie M. Davis, **A GUIDE TO INFORMATION SOURCES FOR READING.** Newark, Delaware: International Reading Association, 1972.

Arden R. Thorum, **INSTRUCTIONAL MATERIALS FOR THE HANDICAPPED.** Salt Lake City, Utah: Olympus Publishing Co., 1976.

Ruth H. Aubrey, **SELECTED FREE MATERIALS FOR CLASSROOM TEACHERS** (5th Edition). Belmont, California: Fearon Publishers, 1975.

Bruce Raskin (Ed.), **THE WHOLE LEARNING CATALOG.** Palo Alto, California: Education Today Co., Inc., 1976.

*Another suggestion is a Comprehensive Membership offered by the International Reading Association (International Reading Association, 800 Barksdale Road, Newark, Delaware). Each year the members receive the equivalent of several hundred dollars worth of material.

INDEX